ACKNOWLEDGEMENT

The mandalas appearing throughout the document were created by Toni Arnon.

PART 1
THEORY

Abraham Maslow devoted much of the last decade of his career to the study of the peak experience. He noted that athletes in the zone, mystics recounting moments of enlightenment, artists when under the influence of their muse, and everyday persons at their ethical and humanistic best appeared to share a common state of consciousness. In synthesizing their reports, he noted that the same B-values were invariably used to capture the spirit of that consciousness (wholeness, beauty, goodness, aliveness, etc.).

What might the world be like if these values dictated human behavior? Maslow posited that humanity would be operating at its optimum. He named that world Eupsychia. He made some brief forays into the world of business and management to promote the spread of these values. His untimely death in 1970 cut short that mission.

This book picks up where Maslow left off. The focus is widened to include any context in which a person or individuals are getting in the way of their own excellence (operating at less than peak) and choose to elevate and illuminate their behaviors.

In Part 1, Maslow's career leading up to and including his study of the peak experience is briefly summarized. The focus is then directed at the peak experience itself. My intention here is to make the case that these experiences are within reach of almost anyone who ventures toward them. Further, in agreement with Maslow, I argue that adopting the B-values in ever more aspects of one's life is the surest, simplest, and safest pathway to better mental health, a more creative life, and increased spiritual aliveness.

1

Maslow's Legacy

This book was written as a guide for individuals and groups who want to "live and grow, become happier and more effective, fulfill themselves, like themselves better, improve in general, and move toward the ideal of perfection, even though they never expect to fully reach that point."

Abraham Maslow, who offered this lofty goal for humankind, died in 1970 at the age of 62. He had accomplished a great deal in his career, most notably sending a wake-up call to the field of psychology, insisting that healthy people—and particularly the most healthy—deserve to be studied and understood as much as those with deficiencies or psychoses.   Still, when reading Maslow's last works, both published and unpublished, one cannot help but feel that his most profound contributions and impact were derailed by death. As Colin Wilson expressed it a quarter-century later, "Maslow has still not come into his own. His significance lies in the future and will become apparent in the 21st century."

Through his research and life experiences, it became obvious to Maslow that the key to a better future for both individuals and society—in all respects—requires tapping more fully into our potential for *wholeness*. This includes ethical behavior, but more so extends to our genius, our joy, our wonder, our appreciation for life's bounties, and our support for one another's growth. This potential for wholeness, he insisted, is innate, yet remains only modestly accessed.

The seeds for Maslow's insights regarding human potential were planted in the summer of 1938, which he spent with the Northern Blackfoot tribe. Maslow was profoundly impressed by the cooperativeness, non-competitiveness, and sharing which Blackfoot people exhibited in their daily lives as cultural norms. He contrasted their generosity and social-mindedness with the greed and egocentricity that were prevalent and often actively promoted in mainstream culture. The Blackfoot culture drew out humanity's best qualities; the western culture did this less well and often frustrated the emergence of these good qualities.

Decades later, Maslow coined the term "Eupsychia" (eu=good; psyche=soul) to refer to any setting in which individuals are encouraged to operate at or close to full potential. In a Eupsychian setting, cultural norms, reward systems, and environmental triggers work together to bring out the wholeness in individuals and groups. In turn, these individuals and groups introduce enhancements within the setting, which catalyze still more individuals and groups to tap into their potentials for wholeness. Eupsychia, Maslow mused, is the Good Society in which Good Persons thrive. Each feeds the other until a critical mass of high-performing people emerges and helps launch humankind's next quantum leap.

There was a natural flowering in Maslow's research and writing from 1938 forward, leading up to this Eupsychian vision for humankind. Let's briefly trace his progression.

The D-Realm

During the 1940s, Maslow developed his popular *hierarchy of needs* framework. Four basic needs, shown in the illustration in red, constitute what he termed the D-realm (D for deficiency). When unsatisfied, there exists the gnawing sensation within us that something essential is missing and must be acquired. When hungry, we must eat; when isolated, we need company. When any of the four levels of need is satisfied, a temporary equilibrium is established at that need-level and persists until some deficiency is again felt there.

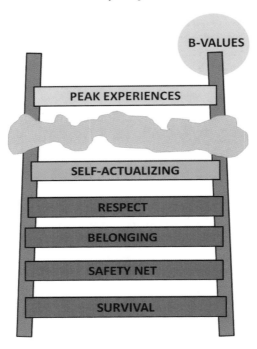

The lowest, most basic need (level one) is to survive. When air is denied, nothing else matters to us than to breathe. When we are freezing, our demands for warmth trump all else. When immediate survival needs are addressed satisfactorily, our focus will rise to the second level on the needs hierarchy. Here, we are motivated to establish a safety net that includes such items as permanent shelter, guaranteed supplies of food and drink, protection from harm, and readily available care when injured or ill.

While both are considered basic needs, immediate survival is *pre-potent* to the need for a safety net. When faced with a life-or-death situation, we are not able to think about longer-range security. Only when free from immediate danger will our motivations again be directed up the hierarchy. However, new threats to survival will instantly bring us crashing back to ground level.

The needs hierarchy dictates our individual lives, as well as the life of the collective. When a community is ravaged by a natural disaster, such as a hurricane or flood, immediate concern of the community-at-large is to satisfy basic survival needs (level one). Only after people are helped to address immediate and short-term survival concerns will attention and resources be redirected to longer-term rebuilding (level two).

With a sufficient safety net in place, individual concerns turn upward to the third basic need: to belong. We are motivated to be part of a family, a friendship circle, a religion or sect, a gang, a community. We do not wish to be isolated and alone. We seek company, at least enough of the time to know we are wanted. Infants denied this connection with a parent or surrogate may get stuck at this level, grow up feeling that they don't belong, and devote their lifetime to seeking and keeping friends and experiencing acute pain when rejected. Similarly, infants denied adequate food can evolve into adults who never can have enough food or anything else they might consume.

Satisfying the need to belong elevates and redirects focus to the highest of the four deficiencies: the need for respect. This translates to the desire to be appreciated by others, to have status, to be viewed as worthwhile. It also encompasses drives for self-esteem and self-confidence. In short, individuals want to feel good about who they are and want others to be impressed by them. One can become sated with food and friendship networks. Yet, for some, there can never be enough applause or praise; they remain perpetually needy at level four.

Much of the resources and activity in affluent societies are devoted to reminding people they don't have enough and need more goods, pleasures, friendships, and status. Meanwhile, in many parts of the world, entire populations can scarcely get beyond the two lowest levels of need. And even in the more affluent nations, far too large pockets of individuals and families remain stuck at these low levels. The resources and activity of the public and philanthropic sectors are largely devoted to addressing the lowest two basic needs.

Need and fear are closely aligned. Thoughts of being needy freely intermingle with those focused on the dreadful circumstances one could find oneself in as a result. A hierarchy of fear, corresponding to Maslow's four-level hierarchy of need, would consist of these elements: fear of dying, fear of suffering, fear of being all alone without support, and fear of one's life being meaningless and purposeless.

Self-Actualization

Free for a brief or prolonged period from D-realm needs and fears, our higher nature rises to the surface. Under such "good conditions," there is a personality shift from deficiency-mindedness to growth-centeredness. As Maslow noted, here "people can be expected to manifest such desirable traits as affection, altruism, friendliness, generosity, honesty, kindness, and trust." They do not need more love or respect from others; rather they demand more of themselves. They give space for their inner being to emerge and light up themselves and their world. They experience the B-alternative (B for being) and function as *self-actualizers*.

These same traits are evident in the D-realm, such as when one cares for one's family or does a favor for a friend. The difference, according to Maslow, is that the underlying motivation in the D-realm—however well disguised—is selfishness; the other person is being *used* to gain more for self. Thus, there is D-love and D-friendliness which can be unfavorably contrasted with B-love and B-friendliness. With the B-alternative, one acts spontaneously and whole-heartedly without one's self in mind. Using the terms of Martin Buber, the D-realm is about I-it experiences whereas the B-alternative is about I-Thou relations. I-it experiences are manipulative; while I-Thou relations are mutually uplifting.

Among the admirable qualities that Maslow associated with self-actualizers, they are:

- More integrated and less split
- More open for experience
- More uniquely themselves
- More spontaneous
- More fully functioning
- More creative
- More humorous
- More ego-transcending
- Less fixated on the D-realm
- More perfectly actualizing their potentialities
- Closer to the core of their being
- More fully human.

Maslow insisted self-actualizers do not constitute an exclusive club. Nearly anyone, given the "good conditions" where D-needs are satisfied, can opt for the B-alternative to thrive and grow. However, he did acknowledge that some—far more than others--were blessed by birth, life circumstance, and predisposition and can more readily and more often overcome the D-needs and self-actualize.   Self-actualizers, as a designation, refer to those men and women who, more frequently than the norm, have the propensity and good fortune to step out of and beyond the D-realm.

The plot thickens.

Peak Experiences

As Maslow considered the lives of famous people throughout history who appeared to be self-actualizers, he noticed that many reported mystical-like experiences. Maslow was not a religious person nor had he previously shown much interest in metaphysics. However, in the mid-1950s, his curiosity and researcher integrity compelled him to delve into these experiences.

He began interviewing college students and others, and discovered that a sizeable portion could report at least one, often several, moments in their lives when they felt they had somehow transcended conventional time and space. They were elsewhere, on a higher plane of being. They were somehow wiser through being in touch with something unexplainable and beyond the ordinary. The triggers and contexts for these *peak experiences* varied, yet their descriptions of the sensations and mental shifts were not only similar to one another but echoed those self-reported by exceptionally creative individuals and sages throughout human history!

Maslow enumerated the common features of the peak experience as the feeling of wonder and awe, great happiness, loss of fear about the future, and an awakened sense of one's own innate abilities. He equated them with "extreme inner health." Maslow noted that these often brief, sometimes more lengthy, experiences delivered a profound and lasting impact. "Reality" could no longer be looked at or interpreted as it had been prior to the experience. The individuals felt infinitely better about their lives and about the world in general. They gained or increased their faith in the ineffable. They also became more acutely sensitized to how far humanity-at-large was from realizing our collective potential.

Maslow described these positive after-effects of a peak experience:

- Therapeutic effects that temporarily or permanently remove neurotic tendencies
- A changed view of oneself in a healthy direction
- A changed view of others and one's relationship with them
- A changed view of the world or parts within it
- Being released for greater spontaneity, creativity, and expressiveness
- A recognition of the importance of peak experiences and the desire to repeat them
- The feeling that life in general is worthwhile, even if it is usually drab, pedestrian, painful, or ungratifying; since beauty, excitement, honesty, play, goodness, truth, and meaningfulness have been demonstrated to exist.

Whereas the D-realm is decidedly human, the B-alternative transcends D-cognition and D-motivation. In the diagram of the needs hierarchy presented earlier, a cloud was placed between self-actualizing and peak experiences. This was intended to convey the mystery attached to the peak experience. It represents the transition from one fundamental type of reality experience to another. One cannot easily extrapolate what a peak experience is like from the clues in the D-realm. As the Austrian artist, Friedrich Hundertwasser, tried to explain, "It was like walking in a dream."

Mozart offered his interpretation: "When I am, as it were, completely myself, entirely alone and of good cheer; it is on such occasions that my ideas flow best and most abundantly. Whence and how they come, I know not; nor can I force them. Nor do I hear in my imagination the parts successively, but I hear them, as it were, all at once." Note the frame of mind: centered, self-contained, and positive. In this receptive mode, Mozart tapped into a mysterious source—which Maslow equated with the B-alternative—where wholeness, completeness, beauty and perfection invaded his being. His gift was to hear what others could not and to gift that music back to the world.

Amy Lowell offered a similar observation regarding the mysterious source of inspiration for her poetry. She wrote: "In answering the question, how are poems made? My instinctive answer is a flat, 'I don't know.' The truth is that there is a little mystery here, and no one is more conscious of it than the poet himself. Let us admit at once that a poet is something like a radio aerial—he is capable of receiving messages on waves of some sort; but he is more than an aerial, for he possesses the capacity of transmuting these messages into those patterns of words we call poems." Receptivity to the unknown was clearly a key to opening the doorway to the B-realm.

The Plateau Experience

Whereas peak experiences are other-worldly and mysterious, Maslow recognized that there was a more mild form of personality transcendence. He called this *the plateau experience*. Self-actualizers could train themselves—through meditation, study, and other spiritual disciplines—to operate at this lofty level on a regular basis and evoke its lesser but still wondrous magic. Being less dramatic and out-of-one's-control than the peak experience, the plateau experience has a conscious, self-observing, witnessing quality. Maslow noted:

> The peak-experience itself can often meaningfully be called a 'little death' and a rebirth in various senses. The less intense plateau experience is more often experienced as pure enjoyment and happiness, as, let's say, in a mother sitting quietly looking, by the hour, at her baby playing, and marveling, wondering, philosophizing, not quite believing. She can experience this as a very pleasant, continuing, contemplative experience rather than as something akin to a climactic explosion which then ends.

Maslow did not place much stake in a society where individuals chased after higher and higher peak experiences. He suspected that such a society could easily collapse in its self-centeredness and disregard for life's challenges within the D-realm. A society founded on cultivating the plateau experience, on the other hand, held great promise. He wrote, "All I wish to do here is to correct the tendency of some to identify experiences of transcendence as only dramatic, orgasmic, transient, 'peaky,' like a moment on the top of Mount Everest. There is also the high plateau, where one can stay 'turned on.'" Maslow explained:

> Peak experiences must be transient, and in fact are transient so far as I can make out. And yet an illumination or an insight remains with the person. He can't really become naïve or innocent again or ignorant again in the same way as he was. He cannot "un-see." He can't become blind again. And yet there must be a language to describe getting use to the conversion or the illumination or to living in the Garden of Eden. Such an awakened person normally proceeds in a B-cognizing way as an everyday kind of thing—certainly, whenever he wishes to. This serene B-cognition or plateau-cognition can come under one's own control. One can turn it off or on as one pleases.

The Good Person

In the final years of his life and career, Maslow made some bold assertions. He argued for a normative—what ought to be—approach to the future of humankind. Social reformers should state clearly what they mean by 'good persons' and promote social action that encourages more like them. He wrote:

> We must have better human beings or else it is quite possible that we may all be wiped out, and even if not wiped out, we will certainly live in tension and anxiety as a species. This Good Person can equally be called the self-evolving person, the fully illuminated or awakened or perspicuous man or women, the fully human person, the self-actualizing person, etc. In any case it is quite clear that no social reforms, no beautiful constitutions or beautiful programs or laws will be of any consequence unless people are healthy enough, evolved enough, strong enough, good enough to understand them and to want to put them into practice in the right way.

Maslow felt he had a good appreciation for the type of individuals society should cultivate and model itself after. These were the self-actualizers, particularly when they were drawing on lessons or insights from their peak and plateau experiences to shape a better life for themselves and the world. He saw them as advanced scouts, as 'superior' people, who knew better than the rest of us what is good, beautiful, and truthful. We should use them, he insisted, as our experts, just as "art collectors will hire art experts to help them with their buying." He echoed the words of Aristotle: What the superior man thinks is good, that is what is *really* good. He went farther: What these superior people value is what I will come to value; and these values will be seen, in time, to be the ultimate values for the whole species.

B-Values

Superior people operate through B-values (B for being). Once experienced, they become addicted to these values and want to go deeper into reality through them. The B-values represent for them the end of the journey of the ego and the portal into what lies ahead. They might wish to stay floating within these abstract values, yet are compelled by both biological needs and worldly attachments to return to the D-realm and be useful to others. In this sense, the D-realm and B-alternative are inextricably linked.

There are 14 B-values. Maslow introduced them as follows:

❖ **WHOLENESS** (unity; integration; tendency to oneness; interconnectedness; simplicity; organization; structure; dichotomy-transcendence; order)

❖ **PERFECTION** (necessity; just-rightness; just-so-ness; inevitability; suitability; justice; completeness; "oughtness")

❖ **COMPLETION** (ending; finality; justice; "it's finished"; fulfillment; *finis* and *telos*: destiny; fate)

❖ **JUSTICE** (fairness; orderliness; lawfulness; "oughtness")

❖ **ALIVENESS** (process; non-deadness; spontaneity; self-regulation; full-functioning)

❖ **RICHNESS** (differentiation; complexity; intricacy)

❖ **SIMPLICITY** (honesty; nakedness; essentiality; abstract, essential, skeletal structure)

- ❖ **BEAUTY** (rightness; form; aliveness; simplicity; richness; wholeness; perfection; completion; uniqueness; honesty)
- ❖ **GOODNESS** (rightness; desirability; oughtness; justice; benevolence; honesty)
- ❖ **UNIQUENESS** (idiosyncrasy; individuality; non-comparability; novelty)
- ❖ **EFFORTLESSNESS** (ease; lack of strain, striving, or difficulty; grace; perfect, beautiful functioning)
- ❖ **PLAYFULNESS** (fun; joy; amusement; gaiety; humor; exuberance; effortlessness)
- ❖ **TRUTH/HONESTY/REALITY** (nakedness; simplicity; richness; oughtness; beauty; pure, clean, and unadulterated; completeness; essentiality)
- ❖ **SELF-SUFFICIENCY** (autonomy; independence; not-needing-other-than-itself-in-order-to-be-itself; self-determining; environment-transcendence; separateness; living by its own laws)

His use of synonyms points to the difficulty in finding the *precise* word to describe any one of these 14 values. Their depth, breadth, and richness ultimately defy labels and definition. They exist at a different dimension than that for which words work well. Paraphrasing William Wordsworth, trying to describe a B-value with one or even a bunch of words is like trying to play a symphony with only a flute.

Maslow's employment of one B-value as a synonym for another (for example, simplicity for truth as well as for beauty) points to their self-sameness at *essence*. As he explained,

> These are not mutually exclusive. They are not separate or distinct, but overlay or fuse with each other. Ultimately they are all *facets* of being rather than *parts* of it. Various aspects will come to the foreground of cognition depending on the operation which has revealed it.

The adoption of the B-values can prove transformative. Most experiences, for example, can be enriched through the introduction of more aliveness and playfulness. Any election campaign can be improved through an insistence on honesty and truthfulness. Any chore can be elevated by aiming for effortlessness and excellence.

Maslow suggested that being deprived of any of the B-values might lead to emotional illness, what he termed *meta-pathology*. Most of the world's populations and society-at-large, unbeknownst to them, might well be suffering from as many as 14 different types of emotional illness or metapathologies. Hence, the challenge for social reformers and world leaders is not simply to help people who are deprived of the four basic needs. It is not nearly enough to stop there. People need guidance to navigate the world via B-values. Otherwise there will be unrecognized and often acute suffering at the meta-psychological level.

Final Years

Likely inspired by Aldous Huxley's novel, *Island*, Maslow pondered what type of culture would emerge if 1,000 self-actualizers were placed on an isolated island. How might their B-values and B-perceptions translate into the ideal society? That society he called Eupsychia. He made use of the term, Eupsychian, as an adjective to distinguish any lifestyle, activity, setting, or community that promotes self-actualization among all participants. While Huxley's island was utopian, Maslow viewed Eupsychia as realizable and worthy of effort to achieve.

Maslow made some unique and well-appreciated contributions to the field of management with his 1965 publication, *Eupsychian Management*. He proposed that self-actualizers operate differently and better in the workplace than those motivated solely by D-needs. They are propelled by meta-needs for creativity, novelty, autonomy, and self-expression (all B-values) which translate to higher performance and increased bottom line for their organizations.

He made brief forays into other domains, such as politics and university life, but his untimely death left explorations of Eupsychia largely incomplete. My aim is to revive interest and advance this exploration. How would Eupsychian candidates shake up the political landscape? How might Eupsychian practices reshape community dialogue? What new strategies would Eupsychian educators employ to inspire their students? It is these and similar questions that I will attempt to address as we proceed.

Maslow set forth his ideas about self-actualizers, peak experiences, B-values, and Eupsychia as "testable propositions." In the D-realm, scientific method offers the best pathway to testing and proof. However, explorations that venture beyond the D-realm must rely on subjective and intuitive evidence. In short, one must switch from on-looker to participatory consciousness and verify propositions directly by living them. This book represents my attempt to put Maslow's ideas to the test, as well as serves as an invitation for you to journey alongside me.

2

Glimpses of Eupsychia

In the simplest sense, this is the sheer enjoyment of the state of gratification, of hope fulfilled and attained, of being there rather than of striving to get there, of having arrived rather than of traveling toward.

Abraham Maslow

Utopias are fictional, Eupsychia is not. Eupsychia represents the upper limits of possibility in any setting, as individual and collective potentials for wholeness come into play. As introduced in the first chapter, the potential for wholeness includes ethical behavior, but more so extends to qualities and values associated with self-actualizers enjoying peak and plateau experiences. Wandering into a Eupsychian setting, we would likely encounter individuals interacting together through the following mindset:

- ❖ Ensuring that whatever gets done has integrity
- ❖ Adding vitality to each and every moment
- ❖ Taking each new situation in stride and with fresh eyes
- ❖ Being playful and caring
- ❖ Bringing the invisible into the light
- ❖ Acting and experiencing through the heart as well as the mind

We would definitely *not* encounter many of these non-Eupsychian, deficient behaviors:

- Operating in ways that are narrow-minded and self-serving
- Going through the motions without drawing the best out of oneself and each other
- Being bogged down due to perceived limitations on resources
- Reacting to situations through negatively critical eyes
- Speaking clichés and truisms without testing their worth

Natural environments are inherently Eupsychian; human-controlled settings unfortunately far less so. When walking on a beach or enjoying a beautiful sunset, it is relatively easy for a least a few moments to rise above the hierarchy of basic needs and experience the world through B-filters. In contrast, when confronted with deadlines or with a new supervisor who is trying to prove herself at your expense, it takes a lot of maturity and discipline to remain whole, graceful, effortless, and open-hearted.

And what is uplifting for some may fail to move or deflate others. A few hours spent in a shopping mall at Christmas time, for example, can evoke the best or the worse in people. Certain times, such as Presidential or local election seasons, can bring out the most noble or the most mean-spirited behaviors.

The focus of this book will draw heavily on the B-values (B for 'Being') that Abraham Maslow enumerated.[1] I suspect that he came up with this list in one or two moments of inspiration. At first and even second glances, they do not appear to be based on an underlying model or a carefully crafted classification system. Yet, as I will explore in successive chapters, consciously or subconsciously Maslow produced a psychological framework far more fascinating than the one he devised for the four basic needs.

Maslow characterized Being-oriented experiences as evoking self-sufficiency, truth, playfulness, effortlessness, uniqueness, goodness, beauty, simplicity, richness, aliveness, justice, completion, perfection, and wholeness. Staying attuned to these values—individually and as a set—can become a self-help agenda and spiritual discipline. I also believe, as Maslow did, that enlivening all settings with ever more of these 14 values represents a universal formula for the good life for individuals, organizations, and communities. True the fourteen are abstract. Yet that contributes to their generative power. The BE-values encompass and transcend the best in life and in all of us. Our best-possible futures will only emerge as more of us—more fully and creatively—integrate these values within personal, familial, and professional relationships and in local and global policies, programs, and cultural norms.

Sabino Canyon

Most weekday mornings, I follow the same ritual. I drive 10 miles to Sabino Canyon in northeast Tucson. There, I don my sweatband, floppy hat, and water belt, do a bit of stretching, and begin a seven-mile roundtrip hike through this oasis in the desert. As I walk, I intentionally cut off as much inner monologue as I can. I welcome in the natural sights and sounds, as well as the crunching of my hiking shoes on the road. I smile and bid 'Good Morning' to the regulars on the trail. I periodically stop and look around at this vast wonderland and offer thanks for making this daily experience possible at this stage in my life.

It is a priceless gift to have this opportunity so close at hand. Tucson is a lovely city with its big sky and with mountain views in all four directions. Its size is manageable, there is lots of sunshine, one does get used to the summer heat, and the diverse population, by and large, is both friendly and free-spirited. Still the option to step away from the traffic and hubbub of urban life to replenish myself each morning within Sabino takes living in Tucson to entirely-other-quality dimensions.

[1] From here forward, I will start using BE-values instead of Being-values or Maslow's abbreviated term, B-values. I feel it is a more evocative and affirmative way to reference the 14 values associated with peak experiences.

The canyon is strikingly beautiful in its simplicity. It is unique: there is no place exactly like this place. Although I walk the same path nearly every day, there are always small surprises. Recently, for example, I came upon a squirrel sitting immobile on a rock chirping mournfully for heaven knows what. I also saw two deer and several roadrunners (the bird variety—we have dozens of the human kind). The people on the trail are respectful and pleasant. Michael, the canyon's unofficial ambassador, greets one and all with "Hello, young man. Hello, young ladies. What a glorious day!" as he jogs by. He has confessed to me that he does not want to make the mistake of by-passing an angel in disguise, so he treats one and all as though they were divine. On some level, of course, he is well aware that we are *all* angels. Michael is also a good source of information on what's current in University of Arizona athletics—riding the waves of success and defeat of local college teams being my enduring D-addiction (D for 'Deficiency').

I can be fully myself in the canyon. Daily excursions to Sabino Canyon serve to align my inner space with the BE-values and the B-perspective. Within this natural setting, the possibility is ripe for a profound mirroring effect. The big sky invites a big mind. The majesty of the mountains invites the majesty of inner being. The outer quiet evokes inner quietness. Outer harmony and peacefulness invites inner harmony and peace.

On the half-hour, tourists and other canyon visitors pile onto open-air trams for a ride through the canyon. The drivers provide an informative lecture about the history of the canyon, the wildlife, the cacti and other vegetation, while pointing out attractive stone formations. I ponder what might be the impact of an alternative tour more meditative in nature. How many visitors might leave the park self-actualizing? Is the US Forest Service that manages the area allowed to promote this B-perspective? If not, why not? If so, then when?

Growth Choices

To BE or not to be, that indeed is the question.

In his classic work, *I and Thou*, Martin Buber observed that the world, as we know it, must always be approached in either one of two ways. The first choice, which he termed the "I-it experience," corresponds to life lived with a Deficiency-orientation. The sense of "Me!" dominates the experience. It is all about "Me!" "Me!" wants this; "Me!" needs that. "Me!" accumulates possessions and never has quite enough. "Me!" seeks status and security and also never has quite enough. "Me!" is ever fearful of not doing what Me is supposed to do.

Buber named the second and much preferred choice: the "I-Thou Relation." As purely felt and lived, there is no sense of "Me!" here. Rather, there is a conscious shift toward full-ness, whole-ness, one-ness, and together-ness. There is an accompanying sense of awesomeness and mystery. This second of Buber's options corresponds to encountering life through a heightened Being-orientation. It is pure Present-ness. Everything seems more alive and aglow with spirit. It is Heaven realized on earth. As Buber contended: "In the pure history of I-it, one can live an orderly life. One can fill every moment with experiencing and using. But in all the seriousness of Truth: whoever lives only this orderly life is *not* fully human."

Being fully human requires frequent Being-experiences. In making the distinction between I-it and I-Thou perspectives, it was not Buber's intention to discount any aspect of human experience. He explained, "One does not have to downgrade the world of the senses as a world of appearances or illusion. There is no world of appearances, there is only the world— which, to be sure, appears twofold to us in accordance with our twofold attitude. Only the spell of separation needs to be broken."

The Bengali philosopher-poet, Rabindranath Tagore, made a similar observation when he wrote:

> Some part of the earth's water becomes rarefied and ascends to the skies. With the movement and music it acquires in those pure heights it then showers down, back to the water of the earth, making it wholesome and fresh. Similarly, part of the mind of humanity rises up out of the world and flies skyward; but this sky-soaring attains completeness only when it has returned to mingle with the earth-bound mind.

We are challenged to marry these two orientations in all that we do, such that one orientation enriches the other in continuous give-and-take. As we bring I-Thou perspectives into play within the spaces of I's and it's, we continually elevate the roles we play and the impacts we can have on the world around us. This is how we evolve as human beings and as a humankind body: not through material progress in the conventional sense, but rather through enlightening matter in both a material and Being sense. Each time any of us acts with B-consciousness, light is added to matter and everyone and everything advances.[2]

Abraham Maslow referred to these enlightened actions as 'growth choices'. He contrasted these with 'regression choices', which keep one running in place (if not backwards) with a Deficiency-orientation. Here is a summary of his arguments in favor of growth choices:

➤ Clinical and experimental evidence teaches us that making growth choices are better in terms of the person's own biological values (less pain, discomfort, anxiety, tension, insomnia, nightmares, indigestion, etc.).

➤ If a person could see all the likely consequences of growth choices versus all the likely consequences of regression choices, and given the option of one set of choices or the other, that person would always (if acting sanely) choose the consequences of growth and reject the consequences of regression.

➤ Growth choices have more evolutionary and survival value when conditions are 'good', i.e., when there are enough resources to go around. Regression choices have intrinsic value only when conditions are 'bad', i.e., when some must survive at the expense of others. However, these bad conditions are much rarer than believed.

---

[2] This is an essential teaching of Kabbalah and other mystical traditions.

- Regression and defense, living at the safety level, amounts to giving up many of the defining characteristics of a healthy human being—such as uniqueness, honesty, goodness, and richness.

- If we were to pick those we most admire, whom we would most like to be like, we would see that they exhibit growth rather than regressive characteristics. In contrast, those we tend to think less well of are those who are regressive and selfish by nature.

Glimpses of the Eupsychian Mindset

In the late 1960s, I got an early taste of a Eupsychian work environment. I was completing my doctorate at the University of California, and taking a few elective courses to broaden my horizons. One of those was An Introduction to Pattern Language, taught by an inspiring and brilliant architecture professor, Christopher Alexander. While the course focused on architectural design solutions, I was trying to figure out how to extend it to urban planning, my primary field of study. I approached Chris after one class, and asked for some time when we might explore together a budding idea. He invited me to meet the next afternoon, a Friday, at his work space in downtown Berkeley.

The office turned out to be in a modest house that had been transformed into his design studio, Christopher Alexander and Associates. The front door was open and the sound of drums and flutes lofted out and drew me into what once must have been a large living room. A dozen or so young professionals and graduate students, creatively attired in the Hippie couture of those experimental times, were celebrating the end of the work week with wine and song. Chris was in the midst of them, and waved to me as I looked around in pleasant shock. How unlike the box-like environment of the management consulting firm in downtown San Francisco, where I was working part time to pay the bills. Chris offered me a glass of wine as we walked into his office. I forgot what we discussed, although I am sure it was inspiring. What was imprinted in my soul was not what we talked about but the realization that work space could—and should—be celebrative and a place I want to be.

Clearly the energy in the design studio was not always one of fun and celebration. This was a Friday afternoon festivity as an end-of-the-work-week release. Still, the signs and energy were there and spoke volumes. This was a creative place, where talent, aesthetics, functionality, integrity, and playfulness all had a home. I was predisposed to see these signs, having spent several months listening to Chris lecture and reading his writing. Often that is the case with Eupsychian places and mindsets: we have the choice and predisposition to recognize them as such, or not. Did everyone who worked in or visited this setting see it through such rose-colored glasses and come away self-actualizing? Probably they did not. However, the possibilities were there.

Some few years later, I was teaching courses in urban planning at the Hebrew University in Jerusalem. At the same time, I was exploring my Jewish roots with a propensity toward the mystical. Jerusalem was clearly the place for this. I engaged with a small group of similarly minded explorers in what we termed 'rabbi hopping'. We scouted around for rabbis who were inspiring to listen to and willing to share their insights and spirituality with Americans with limited Hebrew and non-Orthodox inclinations. Through their classes and excursions to holy sites, I was continually having peak experiences. Between these events, I maintained at a high plateau, which translated in unique ways into my university teaching. I was considered very unconventional and, perhaps because of that, my classes were popular. My intent was for the students to leave the classroom more elevated than when they arrived. This sometimes happened.

I lived just down the street from the home where Martin Buber had resided in the last decades of his life, and often made pilgrimages up the street, stopping in front of the Buber house for a moment or two to take in the vibrations. I made frequent visits to sites considered holy by Jews, Christians, and Muslims, noticing how others approached them as D-tourists or B-seekers. The former absorbed the historic facts and took pictures. The latter seemed profoundly moved; for them, the spirit of Jerusalem triggered Eupsychian frames of mind.

On Thursday evenings, for close to a year, I journeyed into the Hasidic section of Jerusalem to study with a well-known rabbi. The lessons, which were often profound, ended at around one at night. The rabbi and a few of his followers would then crowd into my Volvo station wagon, and we would head south toward Bethlehem, stopping at Rachel's Tomb, There we would join a hundred or so other Hasidim, and pray or meditate throughout the remainder of the night.

According to tradition, Rachel's Tomb is a 'hot spot' at these hours, where and when the presence of God is said to be most acutely felt. Among those in attendance were a small group of rabbis considered to be 'masters of prayer', the ones Jews approach when they have something very important to share with God and want to make certain their messages are delivered. Just before sunset, we would pile into the car and drive back north to the Western Wall. There we would pray and dance—in a circle, Hasidic-style—until the sun came up and the local flock of doves filled the air.

Sitting here in Tucson so many years later, I ponder what could happen if anyone entering Jerusalem—Israelis, Palestinians, other Jews, other Moslems, all Christians, Buddhists, atheists, et al—instantly would become elevated to B-consciousness. Would the threat of terrorist bombs in the market places cease? Probably yes. Would peace conferences held within the walls of the Old City be more productive and enlightened? Probably yes. Could the issue regarding the future of Jerusalem be resolved? Also probably yes.

I had a recent glimpse of a Eupsychian-minded community in action. The location was Recovery Innovations in Phoenix, Arizona. This large nonprofit corporation provides services to thousands of adults with serious mental illness and substance abuse issues, while intentionally remaining focused on the uniqueness and wonder of each individual. Their mission: "to create opportunities and environments that empower people to recover, to succeed in accomplishing their goals, and to reconnect to themselves, others, and meaning and purpose in life." The lyrics of their theme song: "Don't forget to remember you who are, where you came from, where you been thus far. It's so easy for the hard times to leave scars when you forget to remember who you are."

This community of service recipients and service providers achieves extraordinary success through enacting a value system founded on hope, love, choice, mutuality, and respect. These values are reflected in the mission, but also in the design of spaces, roles and opportunities, therapeutic and educational activities, and—most significantly—in the mindsets and relationships formed and nurtured. There are no victims here and no deficits. Recovery Innovations is among the leaders in the mental health arena in their no-restraints policy. The focus of the therapy remains on helping participants remember who they are when at their best, and making decisions and taking actions to be these persons. And we are talking about interactions among thousands of adults here, not just a few dozen. Eupsychian mindsets can be scaled up when a critical number of self-actualizers set out to do this.

Don't Worry, Be Happy

Meher Baba was an Indian mystic and spiritual leader. Deceased now for more than forty years, his teaching and essence continue to guide the hearts and minds of millions of devotees throughout the world—including a number of my good friends. A masterful teacher, he playfully condensed his enormous reservoir of understanding of human nature and Divine consciousness into this single phrase, "Don't Worry, Be Happy."[3] Baba evoked this simple, yet direct instruction when communicating with followers or attempting to awaken the public at large. If you can master just this, he promised, you will have come a very long way.

"Worry" is a placeholder for a broad set of *deficiency-focused* mental habits. These keep us scrambling around in the world, trying to survive and cope with difficulties, while accumulating wealth, friends, and standing. 'Be Happy' is a psychological trigger allowing the escape for a time from the need-based chatter of life. It invites the adoption of a mind set of receptivity and abundance. As we make the shift from worry to happy, we instantly transport ourselves into a more expansive frame of mind. Here, we experience life as lived in and through peak and plateau experiences. It is paradise regained. Our task as transformers—personal, familial, organizational, societal or global—is to ascend in this way and then, as life dictates, descend to apply the Eupsychian frame of mind that has deepened through these experiences. The aim is to make the ordinary extraordinary. This is the only sure pathway for recognizing paradise on earth.

The end goal is "extraordinary being" for ever increasing numbers. Success in approaching this goal depends on personal ascendency, followed by engagement with others to bring peak and plateau experiences into play in more and more venues. This is a shorthand way of describing what happens with any true spiritual journey, any deep organizational transformation, any profound social movement, or any global renaissance—past, current, or future. When happy, centered, and receptive, we instantly ascend and self-actualize. We experience wholeness, simplicity, and beauty. We feel playful and alive. Confronted with life challenges, we do not revert back to deficiency perspectives. Rather, we remain buoyant and add our brilliance to whatever tasks we face alone and with others.

[3] Bobby McFerrin, a follower of Meher Baba, created a popular song from this refrain that won several honors at the 1989 Grammy Awards.

Being-vibrations are stimulated whenever we are inspired to act through BE-values. These values are a set of guideposts for thoughtful action that are readily observable in people who are functioning at their ultimate best for the good of themselves and others. They are also evident in the active and productive lives of the world's most creative, most spiritual, and most authentic individuals and groups—wherever on earth they reside or do their work.

Embracing these 14 BE-values, one aligns with the most psychologically healthy people, with the most saintly and mystical teachers of all religions, and with the most creative artists, scientists, and thinkers our world produces. Who, then, better to change the world than individuals and groups enlivened and motivated to act through these very same BE-values?

The Art of Centering

The Eupsychian frame of mind is well within the reach of anyone so inclined. It is as simple as snuggling into the moment. "Be here now!" is the rallying cry. There truly is no difficulty in shifting from Deficiencies to Being. One just has to do it. Any time I am happy, I am there. Any time I look out at the world or even at my hand with fresh eyes, as if this were the first time I have seen it, I have elevated my perspective.

There is nothing new here. A 4000-year old text on Centering offered 112 simple actions to transcend ordinary perspectives. Here are a few of my favorites:

@ Consider any part of your body as limitlessly spacious.

@ Feel your substance, bones, flesh, and blood, saturated with cosmic essence.

@ Meditate on knowing and not knowing, existing and not existing. Then leave both aside that you may *be*.

@ Whenever satisfaction is found, in whatever act, actualize this.

@ Simply by looking into the blue sky beyond clouds, the serenity.

@ Center on the word, A-U-M, without any A or M.

Gaston Bachelard, a well respected French philosopher, offered this insight regarding making the shift from D to B:

Immensity is within ourselves. It is attached to a sort of expansion of being that life curbs and caution arrests, but which starts again when we are alone. As soon as we become motionless, we are elsewhere; we are dreaming in a world that is immense. Indeed, immensity is the movement of motionless man.

The challenge is not how to enter or stay with a Eupsychian frame of mind; the challenge is how best to make use of what is gained for the continual benefit of self and others. It does take effort to stay immense; it is much easier to shrink back to average size. It is easier to appear conventionally dull than to remain truly alive. We are educated, programmed, and coerced to see our world through self-centric glasses and act accordingly.

It's not a plot. Our world is simply out of kilter. Through these self-centric lenses, we appear to stand apart from each other. As Martin Buber put it, we treat each other as a thing among things in a world of things. Only in very safe situations do we dare to be intimate in the sense of getting out from behind the psychological walls that separate us.

George Harrison of the Beatles had likely removed these glasses and stepped into the B-zone when he wrote: "We are talking about the space between us all… and the people, who hide themselves behind a wall of illusion, and never glimpse the truth. When you've seen beyond yourself, then you may find peace of mind is waiting there. And the time will come when you see that we're all one, and life flows on within you and without you."

Happiness as a Portal

It can really be so simple. I have a need. Let's say I am thirsty. There is a glass of water in front of me, I pick it up, and drink. In this instant, I *am* satisfied. I am need-free. The satisfaction may last only a second or two. Another need or worry might arise. But in this moment of satisfaction, I am happy. I am self-actualizing. We are all hard-wired for this. It would not be so simple or so universal if this were not the case.

This applies to any need, any worry—small or large, personal or shared with others. The moment there is movement toward a resolution, however tiny or dramatic that movement, there is momentary satisfaction, happiness, and centeredness. True, the dramas of Life's pushes and pulls, ups and downs, will soon assert themselves and conspire to draw us back to realities of deficiency. Still we can elevate and add insight to whatever role we are playing within these deficiency-based dramas. We need not lose ourselves completely and worrisomely in neediness.

Following conventional problem-solving scripts practically assures no real change will be sustained or even attempted. For deep and lasting transformations—at individual to global scales—mindsets and corresponding approaches are needed that draw richly and creatively on the 14 BE-values. As I will attempt to demonstrate, this is far easier than one might now imagine.

3

Peak Experiences and the BE-Values

Perhaps my most important finding was the discovery of what I am calling B-values or the intrinsic values of *being*.

Abraham Maslow

I imagine myself inside my head. That is not too difficult. Now I open my eyes a bit wider, and ooze out into the space in front of and all around me. Out here, I no longer sense a border or boundary. I am a different kind of "I" than I was a moment ago inside my head. I feel an exaggerated sense of wholeness, simplicity, aliveness, and self-sufficiency. Ken Wilber offered his version of a similar experience in these words:

> I am no longer on this side of my face looking at the world out there; I simply am the world. I am not in here. I have lost face—and discovered my Original Face, the Kosmos itself. The bird sings, and I am that. The sun rises, and I am that. The moon shines, and I am that, in simple, ever-present awareness.

Out here, in this expanded self-space, I am simulating, although perhaps in a diluted form, what Abraham Maslow referred to as having a "peak experience." Some call it being enlightened. It was during more intensive peak experiences, I believe, that Mozart heard the music of the spheres, Einstein first grasped relativity, great poets are inspired by their muses, and mystics and prophets confront the Creator. This is the body-mind-space occupied by athletes or warriors when in the midst of battle and "in the zone"… as well as where sinners find grace. I call it the Eupsychian frame of mind.

As this short oozing-out exercise aims to suggest, peak experiences need not be considered rare events available to the enlightened or blessed few. They occur as a natural frame of mind whenever we focus our imagination outward rather than inward, do not get lost in thoughts and, instead, reach outward with our sense of self and blend with whatever is there to engage. When in this natural, peaking frame of mind, a subtle quality of wholeness invades experience. The dividing lines that separate and differentiate me from everything and everyone else, as well as my lingering concepts of the Universe, are muted.

While peaking, the experience of self that I recognize and refer to as "distracted me" does not completely disappear, but it is definitely less obtrusive. I stop the monologue with myself and instead seize the opportunity to enjoy an intimate moment with a living Presence all around *and* within me. As the gospel preacher proclaims, "Hallelujah! You were blind, but now you *see*."

Over many years of intentional practice, I have greatly extended the proportion of time I spend outwardly peaking rather than inwardly lost in thought. I consider this a victory. My success is due largely to my skillfulness in ever more quickly recognizing when I have become distracted, knowing that the "distracted me" is always a weak alternative to my "expansive self," and directing myself to ooze back out into the world of direct experience. Fortunately that option is always available—although often it takes longer to catch myself chattering or to give up the chatter. It is a continuous battle or opportunity, depending on how one looks at it.

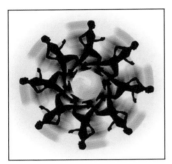

The plight of the "distracted me" was perfectly captured by Lewis Carroll. Early in Alice's adventures in Wonderland, we meet the white rabbit (the persona of a self who is caught up in his or her head) rushing around in near panic, "I'm late, I'm late, for a very important date. No time to say 'Hello! Goodbye!' I'm late, I'm late… I'm late." Later in the book, Alice is running as fast as she possibly can, only to find herself minutes later in the same place beside the same tree. "If you want to get any place else," she is advised, "You have to run twice as fast as that!"

At the quiet center of this mad rushing about, my "expansive self" sits in watch and bides its time. There is a smile on its face. This self is not confused, searching, nor rushed. It appears to have extra-ordinary wisdom that will benefit anyone willing to stop racing and open up to receive it. In a sense, since each of us is that self. So, when expanded, we already possess this timeless wisdom. Yet instead of owning up to our innate brilliance, we opt to be ordinary. It's not really our fault. This is the conventional, normal way to be in the world. In this muted state, we are dependent on the logic, linear thinking that goes on in our head and ignore our genius potential (or, at best, sneak peeks at it when no one is watching).

Maslow's great insight was that through peak experiences we tap into "the soul of the universe" and perceive *its* values rather than those of the distracted me. These BE-values (Beauty, Goodness, Uniqueness, Truth, etc.), according to Maslow, are what has elevated our best art, mathematics, experiments, theories, science, and even business practices from the ordinary toward the "ideal." Giving full form and expression to these BE-values is the ultimate end game of all positive-focused psychotherapies, philosophies, and most religions. I believe it is the only methodology—when embraced by early adopters and ultimately by humanity at large—that will cause a break from conventional reality which seems to be sputtering with a loss of brilliance.

I agree with Maslow. Any individual or group aiming to contribute toward happiness, prosperity, and decency in the world is well-advised first to learn more about and get comfortable with peak experiences and the accompanying BE-values; and then intentionally infuse these values within daily practices and social ventures. This is the surest and simplest way to transform the world at any scale.

This transformation process and what it produces, Maslow labeled Eupsychian (eu = good; psyche = soul). The BE-values are, in Maslow's words, the qualities that animate the "ideally good environment," "the ideally good society," and the truly "good person." All men and women searching for a better world "should heed the words of these good people, follow their lead, be inspired by their deeds, and value what they value."

The Gift of Peaking

Maslow began his exploration of the peak experience with an assumption that this was a state-of-being gifted to a relatively few. However, as he lectured and talked about the experience, he was pleasantly surprised to learn that many of his listeners "got" what he was talking about and recognized these elevated moments from their own lives. Rather than being rare and isolated, Maslow began to view peaking as the lead edge of human consciousness.

Maslow's normative viewpoint was summarized in these words:

It has been my experience through a long line of exploratory investigations going back to the thirties that the healthiest people (or the most creative, or the strongest, or the wisest, or the saintliest) can be used as advanced scouts, or more sensitive perceivers, to tell us less sensitive ones what it is that we value…if I select psychologically healthy humans, what they like is what human beings *will* come to like. Aristotle is pertinent here: "What the superior man thinks is good, that is what is *really* good."

One is simply a better person when peaking. One is mentally healthier. One is more open to creative inspiration. One is more spiritually alive. One is kinder and more compassionate. Could this be the next step in human evolution? What if hundreds, then thousands, then tens of thousands, then hundreds of thousands, then millions, then tens of millions chose—on an ongoing basis—to apply the BE-values to their lives in both small and more profound ways? Thought processes would change. Relationships would change. The work place would change. Politics would change. Education would change. Media reporting would change. Social structures would change. International relationships would change. Religions would change. And all for the better. They would be more beautiful, more just, more playful, more truthful, more whole, more complete, more alive, more unique, simpler yet richer—in short, more perfect.

Where to begin? In Part 2, I introduce a step-by-step process for instilling BE-value into any life situation where deficiencies are recognized and the desire exists to eliminate them. Any situation—private or public, individual or team, at any scale—is fair game for this process. My testable hypothesis is that if we allow the spirit of any of the 14 BE-values to enter and flavor our consciousness, then perceive, think, and speak from this enriched perspective, we will be rewarded with insights and fresh approaches to the situation. In short, we will be operating at our creative peak.

The suggested process represents a radical shift from traditional problem-solving approaches. One is asked to intentionally shift from the perspective of the "distracted me" to that of the "expanded self." This is accomplished by adopting the persona of a BE-value. So, I take a break from being Barry and instead opt to embrace the spirit of, say, Aliveness, and approach the problem from this more lofty and animated perspective. Or as an elite-team of problem-solvers, we agree to drop our personas and instead become a temporary cast that includes Aliveness, Wholeness, Justice, and Effortlessness. We apply our BE-value lenses to the problem and allow our individual and collective genius to point the way.

As Maslow suggested, "Peak experiences are states in which striving, interfering, and active controlling diminish, thereby permitting non-interfering, receptive, Taoist perception, thereby diminishing the effect of the perceiver upon the percept. Therefore, truer knowledge of some things may be expected." So let's give it a try. Let's see what truer knowledge can lend to our individual and group approaches to almost anything where we recognize an opportunity to elevate ourselves and the situation at hand.

4

BE-Value Psychology

> We have come to the point in biological history where we are now responsible for our
> own evolution. We have become self-evolvers. Evolution means selecting and
> therefore choosing and deciding, and this means valuing.
>
> Abraham Maslow

I believe it is not only possible but necessary for ever-expanding numbers of individuals
throughout the world to adopt BE-value behaviors as their guiding ethic. Whenever they sense
that they are operating at less than their best—in effect, getting in the way of their own
brilliance—they will know to attribute this to some poorly executed BE-value and take instant
action to embrace more of that value.

Here is a simple example. I was invited last month to spend the day working with the faculty of
the school of nursing at a university in northern California. They had recently implemented a
new curriculum with a new guiding philosophy and were getting mixed responses from faculty
members. I was asked to speak about program and student evaluation. I admit to knowing a lot
about evaluation practice, but virtually nothing about nursing curricula. I also promote a non-
traditional approach to evaluation that favors discovery rather than evidence gathering. As I
was preparing for the event, I found myself imagining some faculty member with a research
bent standing up mid-way through the day and challenge my credibility. "Sir, this does not make
sense for us and is not helpful!"

Being seeped in BE-value psychology, I immediately recognized that I was slipping down
through my imagination into the D-world. In hierarchical terms, I was back at level four, fearing
the loss of respect. What was that all about? Did I really, truly care if these unknown faculty
respect me? Could I risk the embarrassment and ego blow of being challenged by a peer
evaluator? Enough of that nonsense. I decided, with barely a few seconds of thought, that I
was taking the wrong approach and evoked the spirit of Playfulness. Instead of lecturing on my
approach and seeking approval, I created the opportunity for the faculty to spend most of the
day learning how to play as evaluators with an on-line evaluation tool I customized for them.
Needless to say, the day was a big success. I received only one feeble challenge that I easily
disposed of. The day was orchestrated on my terms, with my values. As it should have been. I
was their guest.

Hermetic Principles

According to legend, thousands of years ago in ancient Egypt there lived a sage called Hermes
Trismegistus. He was reported according to some mythology to have been the teacher of
Abraham during the latter's sojourn into Egypt. The teachings attributed to Hermes have

passed down through the ages as hermetic philosophy. They include his exposition of some principles germane to BE-value psychology.

Hermes taught: The world is mind. To change the world, you must first change your mind. This applies to problems large and small.

Everywhere we see and experience polarities. For every plus, there is its minus; and vice versa. Further, the two poles always have gender: one feminine and one masculine, one yin and one yang, one nurturing and one action oriented.

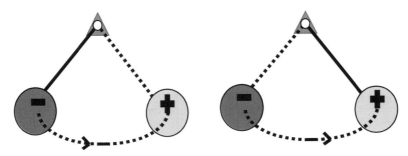

The world does not remain stationary at one pole. Upon reaching either pole, events will shift such that energies are drawn away from this pole (positive or negative) back toward the other, much like the movement of a pendulum.

Such is the way of life. We find evidence of the swings all around us. "Good things don't last; all good things come to an end." "Hang in there, things will change for the better." "The country has moved too far to the political right; now it is adjusting to the left." "We are finally seeing more women in positions of authority." Periods of inward contemplation are followed by more active periods of social action, leading to more contemplative practices, etc.

Each paired pole has its unique vibration. Aliveness (+), for example, feels very different to the mind and body than feeling bored or robotic (-). Playfulness (+) feels distinctly different from cheerlessness (-). Aliveness and playfulness are buoyant and expansive. Feeling bored or cheerless, by contrast, are gravity-bent and restrictive. No two positive poles are exactly alike in vibration. Aliveness does not feel exactly like Playfulness, Simplicity, or Beauty. However each of the 14 BE-values, when embodied, evokes feelings of centeredness, mindfulness, and radical appreciation; while the absence of any of them leaves a "hole" in the psyche that plays out through endless variations of distraction and deficiency.

Now, for the punch line: Life must necessarily move back and forth between any two matched poles, from negative to positive to negative, etc. However, since mind rules over matter, if one can hold and intently focus mental energy at a positive pole, the swing toward the negative can be slowed down and stopped short of full swing. So, as in the illustration below, instead of swinging all the way to red, life stops at orange and returns from there for more yellow. Orange becomes the "negative" pole instead of red, and life is lived at the plateau and is exceedingly more positive.

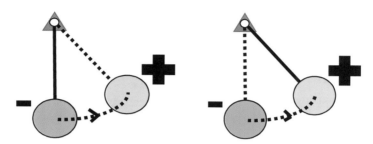

As expressed by the Hermetic philosophy, "To destroy an undesirable rate of mental vibration, concentrate on the opposite pole of the one which you choose to suppress. Kill out the undesirable by changing its polarity. Simply 'refuse' to allow yourself to be swung back and forth by the mental pendulum of mood and emotion. Take command and give the orders."

The Dream

The Dalai Lama captured this universal understanding with these simple words:

> If a room is too hot, there is no way to reduce the heat but to introduce cold. Just as heat and cold oppose each other, so too do opposing mental stares, pure and impure. To the extent you develop one, the other decreases. Therefore, it is possible to remove faulty states of mind. Antidotes exist. When, in your practice, you become accustomed to correct attitudes, faulty states of mind naturally diminish until finally they are extinguished.

Following the same, habitual mental patterns and associated problem-solving scripts will keep the world swinging back toward red. I am reminded of a part of the Gestalt credo of Fritz Perls. "A thousand plastic flowers don't make a desert bloom. A thousand empty faces don't fill an empty room." I am also reminded of the lyrics of a popular 1968 song by Melanie Safka:

> If I had a dream I would fill a hall
> And tell all the people tear down the wall
> That keeps you from being a part of it all
> Cause you got to get close to it all

I have a similar dream. For deep and lasting transformations—for individuals, at work places, and at organizational to national to global scales—problem-solving attitudes and approaches are needed that use yellow mental energy (the spirit of BE-values) to produce orange (more enlightened and compassionate solutions). My intention is to show clearly and simply how to cultivate these attitudes and apply them to whatever problem areas one chooses to tackle, alone and with others.

Faith Matters

It is near impossible to dwell at the plateau and not have faith in something beyond. This is not a question of *believing* in something beyond. It is a *knowing* process. It is faith grounded in direct experience.

Paramahansa Yogananda, one of a line of exalted gurus featured on the cover of the Beatles album Sergeant Pepper's Lonely Heart Club Band, used the term "God" to point to this something beyond. I am also very comfortable with this term, although I can understand why some resist its use. Yogananda wrote:

> I suggest you wrest your mind from the mirage of the senses and habit. Why be deluded like that? I am pointing out to you a Land more beautiful than anything here can ever be. I am telling you of a Happiness that will intoxicate you night and day–you won't need sense temptations to enthrall you. Discipline your mind and your body. Control your senses. Banish the spiritual ignorance that makes you think this mortal life is *real*. Find God!

The Hebrew words for "faith" and "truth" share a common root. For plateau-dwellers, faith is not something accepted because someone told us to believe. The God that I have faith in is as present to me as the air I breathe and the thoughts I think. Just like the discovery of any other truth, I find God by looking for God and realizing, as Abraham Heschel puts it, that God has been looking for me. Rabbi Nachman perhaps said it best: "Every something is infused with God and surrounded by God. There is a thin veil separating one from the other. This cannot be known by knowing; but it can be "faithed" by "faithing" passed and through it."

I have benefitted from the writings and direct lessons of literally hundreds of spiritual guides, some famous and some obscure. I look over at my bookcase and realize that I have read, re-read, marked up, reflected on, and practiced much of what is in these books. And yet it all comes down to these 14 values, experienced and lived. The rest follows. Peak experiences will happen. Insights will be commonplace. Happiness and joy are certainties. The something beyond will make itself known to you. And you will be optimally positioned to self-evolve and be a positive force for radical change in the world.

What about love, compassion, and other positive qualities? I submit that the 14 are sufficient to capture them all. Much as the primary colors (red, yellow, and blue), coupled with black and white, represent all the essentials for the painter's palette, the 14 BE-values combine to produce all the soul and spirit needs. Isn't love, for example, adequately expressed and experienced through wholeness, completion, truthfulness, goodness, aliveness, beauty, and so on? Add faith to the mix and you've got it all nicely ready for execution.

PART 2

PRACTICE

In this next section, a process I call BE-value exploration is presented in detail. It consists of five steps that guide an individual or team from a challenge to inspired action items for tackling it. This process was not designed for "technical" challenges that involve moving physical components or electronic bits into new configurations. It works exceeding well, as you will discover with practice, for most situations where individuals (yourself) or teams are performing at less than peak and intend to do something about that.

5

BE-Value Explorations

> After the insight or the great conversion, or the great mystic experience, or the great illumination, or the great full awakening, one can calm down as the novelty disappears, and as one gets used to good things, live casually in heaven and be on easy terms with the eternal and the infinite.
>
> Abraham Maslow

What is proposed here is a radical approach to individual or group problem-solving. The problem-solvers are requested to give up their chairs and invite Be-values to take their place. So, for example, instead of Jack and Marie working on a challenge, we have the spirits of Aliveness and Self-Sufficiency providing the creative input. Jack is playing the role of Aliveness. Marie is performing as Self-Sufficiency. So literally they have not given up their place at the table. The intent is that they have given up their self-identities for the moment. Once Jack-as-Aliveness and Marie-as-Self-Sufficiency have provided their wisdom, it will be up to Jack-as-Jack and Marie-as-Marie to assess the worthiness of the input and act accordingly.

Here is the reasoning behind the role playing: The solution space of each and every personal or people-centered challenge can be enhanced and elevated—often dramatically—through the infusion of more BE-value. Each increase in dosage of BE-value translates almost immediately to improved mental health, increased happiness, greater creativity, and heighted aliveness. So much can be gained, and so little lost, by taking a breather from the typical approaches to problem-solving and view any challenge through the expansive perspective of the BE-values.

In this chapter, I will present a process that I have found really effective for generating highly appreciated BE-value solutions. The process, BE-value exploration, entails five sequential steps that result in dramatic changes for the better—often with relatively modest effort. Any of these steps can be skipped or rushed through and benefits will still be derived. However, devoting just a few minutes of full attention to each element invariably produces deep, inspired and welcomed results. Supporting tools and sufficient guidance are provided in this and subsequent chapters to allow faithful replication of the process. Borrowing a commercial slogan that still brings a grin: "Try it, you'll like it!"

The Five-Step Process

▽	STEP	TOOL	INDIV	TEAM
1	Zero-In on the Challenge	Zero-In Exercise	10 min	20 min
2	Select the BE-value to Role Play	Deficiency Meter	10 min	10 min
3	Get into Character	BE-Value Script	15 min	20 min
4	Respond with Inspiration	Inspiration Sheet	15 min	15 min
5	Reality Check	Discussion Guide	15 min	30 min

As this chart illustrates, each of the five steps has a corresponding tool that is used to execute it. When individuals explore issues on their own, roughly an hour should be enough to complete the process and discover immediate ways for enriching their personal or professional lives. It takes an extra hour for groups to complete the process, to allow for discussion, sharing, and consensus building.

Step 1. Zero-In on the Challenge

Albert Einstein once mused, "If I had only one hour to save the world, I would spend fifty-five minutes defining the problem, and only five minutes finding the solution." This may be a bit extreme. Almost any challenge statement as initially expressed can be improved in five or ten minutes (not 55) through a bit of *depth probing*. The aim is to reframe the challenge in a way that gets more to the root of what's wrong and what what's needed to make it right.

For example, let's say that the initial statement is "How can we get the members of the House of Representatives to stop posturing and do what is in the best interest of the country?" With a bit of depth probing, we might land on this re-statement: "What would it take for the House of Representatives to become a model for the nation and world of wisdom and compassion in action?"

The technique is to ask oneself a "Why?" question, followed with some clarifying "What?" question, and then a second "Why?" question to get closer to the heart of the challenge being addressed. The resulting re-statement of the challenge will feel somehow more open to free and elevated exploration. The solutions that then result as one proceeds with the remaining four steps of the process will be more authentic and generative.

The tool, Zero-In Exercise, guides you through three activities leading to the re-stated challenge. For each activity, four optional ways to pose the next "Why?" or "What?" question are offered. Usually one of these options will jump out as the best way to frame the question. If none of the four works for you, frame the question in a way that does work.

The aim is to get beneath the words themselves and closer to the heart of the matter. Just a small shift in the way the challenge is posed can open you up to some really interesting possibilities that you might easily have missed by sticking to the original wording.

When doing this first step as a group activity, it is ideal to make use of a computer projection system. One person servers as both the facilitator and recorder and is also free to offer input. The trick is to encourage input from all the participants and still synthesize this feedback and reach consensus in a reasonably short period of time. An experienced facilitator should have no problem in moving a group through this step in around 20 minutes. It is a valuable process in its own right as it gets the participants sharing what matters to them.

Here are three examples of completed exercises.

Zero-In Exercise

1. What is the challenge (problem, opportunity, design) that we want to address creatively?

CHALLENGE AS PRESENTED: How can we overcome the resistance of our senior staff to the proposed changes?

2. Pick one of these four WHY questions (mark the box with an X). Ask this question about the challenge above. Write your answer in the space provided.

X   Why is the current situation the way it is?   ☐ Why isn't it being changed already?
☐   Why is it worth trying to make a change?   ☐ Why is change possible?

RESPONSE TO WHY QUESTION: The senior staff feel comfortable with current procedures. They have seen other management innovations come and go and don't want to subject themselves and others to this process yet again.

3. Now pick one of these four WHAT questions (mark the box with an X). Ask this question about the challenge above. Write your answer in the space provided.

☐   What is interesting about this response?   ☐ What would happen if changes were made?
X   What change might make a real difference?   ☐ What has to be given up for changes to happen?

RESPONSE TO WHAT QUESTION: Give them key roles during the roll-out process. Let them be the first ones to pilot the procedures. And then assign them as trainers or mentors to the more junior staff.

4. Ask another WHY question (mark the box with an X). Ask this question about the response above. Write your answer in the space provided.

☐   Why is the current situation the way it is?   ☐ Why isn't it being changed already?
X   Why is it worth trying to make a change?   ☐ Why is change possible?

RESPONSE TO WHY QUESTION: It will help insure ownership in the procedures rather than having these procedures be seen as something imposed on them from above.

5. Now re-write your challenge statement to reflect your best thinking in the above response:

RE-STATED CHALLENGE: What actions will insure full ownership for the senior staff in the proposed changes?

Is it clear why the revised statement will kick-off a richer and more productive exploration?

Zero-In Exercise

1. What is the challenge (problem, opportunity, design) that we want to address creatively?

CHALLENGE AS PRESENTED: How can I quiet my chattering mind?

2. Pick one of these four WHY questions (mark the box with an X). Ask this question about the challenge above. Write your answer in the space provided.

- ☐ Why is the current situation the way it is?
- **X** Why is it worth trying to make a change?
- ☐ Why isn't it being changed already?
- ☐ Why is change possible?

RESPONSE TO WHY QUESTION: Most of the time the chattering involves either replaying some previous event or anticipating some upcoming event—including fictional ones that I know can never happen. It is such an enormous waste of energy with so little return.

3. Now pick one of these four WHAT questions (mark the box with an X). Ask this question about the challenge above. Write your answer in the space provided.

- ☐ What is interesting about this response?
- ☐ What change might make a real difference?
- **X** What would happen if changes were made?
- ☐ What has to be given up for changes to happen?

RESPONSE TO WHAT QUESTION: I would be more peaceful and more mindful of what is happening all around me. Objects would be clearer, food taste better, people more unique and more interesting, my ideas more honest and truthful, and I would just feel like a better person.

4. Ask another WHY question (mark the box with an X). Ask this question about the response above. Write your answer in the space provided.

- ☐ Why is the current situation the way it is?
- **X** Why is it worth trying to make a change?
- ☐ Why isn't it being changed already?
- ☐ Why is change possible?

RESPONSE TO WHY QUESTION: We all have this potential to be perfect. I can't tell you what that means, but I feel it in heart and soul. I know when I am moving in the right direction and have no doubts about it. I feel centered and alive.

5. Now re-write your challenge statement to reflect your best thinking in the above response:

RE-STATED CHALLENGE: How can I center myself and remain centered in more life situations?

Is it clear why the revised statement will kick-off a richer and more productive exploration?

BKIBEL 2014

Zero-In Exercise

1. What is the challenge (problem, opportunity, design) that we want to address creatively?

CHALLENGE AS PRESENTED: How can we get more teens to participate in our after-school youth program?

2. Pick one of these four WHY questions (mark the box with an X). Ask this question about the challenge above. Write your answer in the space provided.

- ☐ Why is the current situation the way it is?
- X Why is it worth trying to make a change?
- ☐ Why isn't it being changed already?
- ☐ Why is change possible?

RESPONSE TO WHY QUESTION: We offer a safe place where teens can get help with homework, participate in Bible studies or life skills development, engage in sports or computer games or arts programs, or just hang out with friends. It enriches their lives and, to repeat, it provides safety.

3. Now pick one of these four WHAT questions (mark the box with an X). Ask this question about the challenge above. Write your answer in the space provided.

- X What is interesting about this response?
- ☐ What change might make a real difference?
- ☐ What would happen if changes were made?
- ☐ What has to be given up for changes to happen?

RESPONSE TO WHAT QUESTION: We are clear about the advantages of what we offer, but obviously the message is not getting out in a convincing way to the teens we hope to reach.

4. Ask another WHY question (mark the box with an X). Ask this question about the response above. Write your answer in the space provided.

- X Why is the current situation the way it is?
- ☐ Why is it worth trying to make a change?
- ☐ Why isn't it being changed already?
- ☐ Why is change possible?

RESPONSE TO WHY QUESTION: They think it will feel like just more hours of school added to their day. This is simply not the case. Just ask the kids already in our program. They have a wonderful time here and look forward to coming.

5. Now re-write your challenge statement to reflect your best thinking in the above response:

RE-STATED CHALLENGE: How might we train and encourage our current participants to serve as champions for our after-school program?

Is it clear why the revised statement will kick-off a richer and more productive exploration?

BKIBEL 2014

Step 2. Select the BE-value to Role Play

A **Deficiency Meter** is next used to reflect on the setting surrounding the re-stated challenge and pinpoint the BE-value to use for inspiration. If there are multiple participants, each individual will use the meter to determine which of the 14 BE-values he or she will embrace in the process. Several persons may wind up with the same BE-value, or a diverse cast of BE-values may enter the play.

There are two versions of the Deficiency Meter. These versions, Deficiency Meter (ME) and Deficiency Meter (WE) appear on the next two pages. The only difference is the use of singulars versus plurals in the wording of the items. Deficiency Meter (ME) is used for solo challenges (i.e., when an individual aims to improve a situation alone). Deficiency Meter (WE) is used when it is a team or group challenge (i.e., it is *our* challenge, rather than *my* challenge).

For this tool, each of the 14 BE-values has a corresponding question stated as a deficiency to be addressed. As examples, the deficiency question for Beauty: "Does my space fail to grab and hold attention? The question for Wholeness: "Is the prevailing mindset divisive and fragmented?" The question of Playfulness: "Have I become too weighted down and joyless?"

A simple rating scheme is used to answer each of the 14 deficiency questions:

- A rating of 0 is assigned to any of the 14 BE-values where its deficiency question can be answered "No, this is not a problem with my challenge."

- A rating of 1 is assigned if the answer is, "A bit. This is true to a limited extent."

- A rating of 2 corresponds to this answer, "Yes. This is true all or most of the time."

- A severe rating of 3 matches the answer, "Absolutely. This is a truly bad situation that has got to be fixed."

Based on the 14 ratings, one of the BE-values is selected for the role play. Since the BE-values are all facets of the same peak experience, working with any one of them tends to bring several others into play. For example, if Wholeness is selected for the role play, it is likely that Completion and Perfection will also be "speaking their minds."

Still, for maximum impact, it makes most sense to select a BE-value with a corresponding deficiency rating of 3 or 2. When there are multiple options meeting this criterion, it is best to trust one's intuition regarding which BE-value is most likely to prove transformative if applied to the challenge. To illustrate, a participant trying to decide between Justice and Effortlessness might conclude, "I can already see how infusing Justice into the setting will have an immediate and profound impact on the challenge. So I will work with that BE-value."

Deficiency Meter (ME)

What is the challenge (problem, opportunity, design) that I want to address creatively?

CHALLENGE: How can I center myself and remain centered in more life situations?

INSTRUCTIONS: RATE each of the 14 deficiencies as they relate to the challenge using this rating scale:

- **0** No. This is not a problem with our challenge.
- **1** A bit. This is true to a limited extent.
- **2** Yes. This is true most or all of the time.
- **3** Absolutely! This is a truly bad situation that has got to be fixed.

DEFICIENCY TO ADDRESS	RATING		BE-VALUE
Is my success overly dependent on the actions of others?	0	>	SELF-SUFFICIENCY
Is my viewpoint too fixed and limiting?	1	>	TRUTHFULNESS
Have I become too weighted down and joyless?	1	>	PLAYFULNESS
Am I feeling stressed and overloaded?	0	>	EFFORTLESSNESS
Is there too much sameness and predictability to my approach?	2	>	UNIQUENESS
Am I acting in ways that are harmful or hurtful?	0	>	GOODNESS
Does the space I am creating fail to grab and hold attention?	1	>	BEAUTY
Have things become overly complicated and cluttered?	1	>	SIMPLICITY
Is the situation one-dimensional?	2	>	RICHNESS
Is there an absence of positive energy and excitement?	1	>	ALIVENESS
Am I contributing to an uneven and unfair playing field?	0	>	JUSTICE
Does it feel like something important is missing?	3	>	COMPLETION
Are results uninspired and is the potential unrealized?	2	>	PERFECTION
Is my mindset divisive and fragmented?	1	>	WHOLENESS

Based on these ratings, which BE-value will I draw on for inspiration?	Completion

What will be gained by injecting more of the spirit of this BE-value into the situation? If I can discover what keeps me from being centered and add that missing element into all of my actions, I will definitely have achieved my objective.

BKIBEL 2014

35

Deficiency Meter (WE)

What is the challenge (problem, opportunity, design) that we want to address creatively?

CHALLENGE: What actions will insure full ownership for the senior staff in the proposed changes?

INSTRUCTIONS: RATE each of the 14 deficiencies as they relate to the challenge using this rating scale:

- **0** No. This is not a problem with our challenge.
- **1** A bit. This is true to a limited extent.
- **2** Yes. This is true most or all of the time.
- **3** Absolutely! This is a truly bad situation that has got to be fixed.

DEFICIENCY TO ADDRESS	RATING		BE-VALUE
Is our success overly dependent on the actions of outsiders?	1	>	SELF-SUFFICIENCY
Is our viewpoint too fixed and limiting?	2	>	TRUTHFULNESS
Have we become too weighted down and joyless?	2	>	PLAYFULNESS
Are we feeling stressed and overloaded?	2	>	EFFORTLESSNESS
Is there too much sameness and predictability to our approach?	3	>	UNIQUENESS
Are we acting in ways that are harmful or hurtful?	1	>	GOODNESS
Does the space we are creating fail to grab and hold attention?	1	>	BEAUTY
Have things become overly complicated and cluttered?	2	>	SIMPLICITY
Is the situation one-dimensional?	1	>	RICHNESS
Is there an absence of positive energy and excitement?	3	>	ALIVENESS
Are we contributing to an uneven and unfair playing field?	0	>	JUSTICE
Does it feel like something important is missing?	2	>	COMPLETION
Are results uninspired and is the potential unrealized?	3	>	PERFECTION
Is our mindset divisive and fragmented?	3	>	WHOLENESS

Based on these ratings, which BE-value will I draw on for inspiration? Aliveness

What will be gained by injecting more of the spirit of this BE-value into the situation? There will be more enthusiasm as well as more trust in the potential of these changes.

NOTE: When doing the five-step process alone, you might choose to repeat the process with a second or even third BE-value after completing it with a first choice. This will result in a more diverse set of solution options for moving forward to address the challenge.

Step 3. Get Into Character

For this step and the one that follows, each participant is challenged to become more like their selected BE-value and less like themselves. Instead of being Jim, for example, Jim is aiming to be Jim-as-Playfulness—the BE-value he selected in the previous step. Jim is being invited to embody (role play) that BE-value.

How will Jim benefit from this somewhat bizarre activity? He has recognized that the current situation lacks sufficient Playfulness. That is why he rated it a 3 on the Deficiency Meter. Jim could simply say, "Okay, let me brainstorm some ideas for making the situation more playful." He will likely come up with some familiar ideas, drawn from his memory bank. He is less likely to draw on his innate and untapped brilliance.

Instead, we want Jim to enjoy and benefit from a peak experience. As our mantra goes, "when you peak, you are more mentally healthy, more creative, and more spiritually alive." In this specific example, Playfulness is the entry point out of the D-world (D for deficiency) and into the BE-world of peak experiences. As Jim embraces the spirit of Playfulness, his mind and heart will open to options that he will find more interesting and generative than those his cleverness would have produced. This, of course, is a claim that Jim will have to verify for himself.

The first step to embrace a BE-value as one's own is to relax. I take a few deep breaths and declare the intention. "I aim to be Playfulness!" Or, "I aim to be Truthfulness!" The BE-values are, by their very nature, stress-free and expansive. So, to embody any one of them, I have to open up and ooze into the surrounding environment. The added benefit of this relaxing exercise is that it takes my mind away from whatever it has been chattering about in Steps 1 and 2; and refocuses it on my selected BE-value. I don't want to get too relaxed, for that might get me out of the character of that BE-value. The aim is to match and align my bodymind with the BE-value. I want to be able to say to myself or others, with some conviction, that "Right now, I am not Barry-as-Barry. I *am* Barry-as-Truthfulness!"

The BE-value script matching the selected BE-value is used to enter into the spirit of the space represented by that value. The complete set of 14 scripts is provided in the Resources section (Part 3). Each script has three components. Intimations, Reading, and Core Behaviors

Intimations: Staying relaxed, the next challenge is to draw on "sense memory." I search for examples I can identify with that get me further into the spirit of my BE-value. To help with this, a set of five examples have been developed for each BE-value. These appear on the top part of the BE-value script.

As an example, for Aliveness the intimations offered are:

- ❖ Waking up in the morning and raring to get started with the day.
- ❖ Gazelles leaping across an open field.
- ❖ An active volcano.
- ❖ A butterfly emerging from the chrysalis.
- ❖ An excited audience applauding a wonderful performance.

I picture myself in the midst of each of these examples. I aim to embrace and own the aliveness of that experience. How do I see the world differently as a gazelle or a volcano? How does Aliveness move through space? How does Aliveness make itself known in the world?

For a moment, I might switch to another BE-value and note the differences in the way that I relate to the world. For example, as Playfulness, how does my morning hike differ from that same activity when being Aliveness? As I nuance the differences between being playful and being alive, I come to appreciate Aliveness in a richer way. This is not as easy an exercise as relaxing. However, it can be very entertaining and informative. With experience and practice, it gets ever easier to slip into one of the BE-values and sense the world through this persona.

I also find it helpful to travel in my mind to a place where that BE-value is at home. For example, when I want to be Barry-as-Beauty, I mind-travel to the seashore or to Sabino Canyon and "become" that place. As Perfection, I am a smiling Buddha floating in endlessness. As Richness, I enter a Starbucks coffeehouse and become the aromas. For some BE-values, it is easier to use a standout experience rather than a place. As Justice, for example, I travel to the Lincoln Memorial as Martin Luther King is delivering his "I have a Dream" speech, and become the words and the sentiments behind them. As Playfulness, I become a puppy or kitten or penguin at play.

The aim is to really own the selected BE-value. If I am alone, I simply say aloud, "I am Goodness!" Or, "I am Perfection!" This is not a name I call myself, this is exactly who I am right now. In a group, we might enjoy a playful exercise. Each participant creates a sign or sticker that identifies the BE-value that he or she is embodying. The participants take turns introducing themselves as their target BE-value and engaging others in the room as their BE-value. For example, "I am Goodness. It feels really good to be here with you all this morning. And it is especially nice to see Richness sitting over there. How are you feeling this morning?"

Reading: A short reading has been prepared for each of the 14 BE-values. It is written in the first-person singular. As one reads, the goal is to act as if one is speaking one's own truth. The reading consists of a few small paragraphs, each intended to get the reader deeper into the spirit of the BE-value it represents. It is not critical for the reader to agree with every single word in the script. The purpose is to use the script for deeper immersion in the BE-value.

If this is a group exercise and more than one person has selected the same BE-value, each should still do the reading and subsequent inspiration exercises alone. They will share results in Step 5.

Core Behaviors: As a final check to see how deeply the participant has identified with the BE-value, three core behaviors are offered. These appear on the bottom of the script as "I statements." For example, if the selected BE-value is Aliveness, the corresponding core behaviors are:

☐ There is a lot of passion behind everything I do.

☐ I enjoy being spontaneous and surprising others.

☐ When I get excited about something, I throw a lot of energy into it.

Hopefully the participant can mentally check each of the three boxes indicating complete identification with these core behaviors. This is, of course, not critical. However, if the participant cannot embrace any of the three behaviors at this moment, it likely means that there is resistance to embracing the BE-value. If that is the case, I advice taking a few deep breaths and returning briefly to the intimations for immersion.

Step 4. Respond with Inspiration

Having identified the BE-value that is causing the current context to be less than ideal, and having embodied the spirit of that value, each individual takes a blank Inspiration Sheet corresponding to the selected BE-value. These are available in the Resources section on the page directly following the BE-script. On it, the re-stated challenge is written.

The problem-solver now enters that content in her or his mind's eye and imagines what can be done to immediately elevate it. The participant lists two or three actions that can be taken or at least started to address the challenge. The idea is not to overwrite, but rather just get down enough words so each inspiration is not lost. After writing these down, a few moments is spent picturing the results of each when fully executed. It should bring a smile or a nod of approval, or both.

An example of a completed sheet based on is offered on the next page. In this example, Sonya, as Simplicity, "looks around" her work environment. She instantly comes up with a way to give added visibility to the vision of the organization. She goes over the wording of her organization's mission statement and immediately rewords it in her mind so that it really says what the organization values and does. Logging on—in her mind—to the company's website, Sonya-as-Simplicity is surprised at its confusion and clutter. She reorganizes it in her head, dropping several features and totally redesigning the home page.

INSPIRATION SHEET
BE-Value: **SIMPLICITY**

Re-Stated Challenge: *How can we better align the day-to-day work of our organization with our five-year vision of success?*

Inspiration #1: *Start every morning by reading our vision statement and drawing a quick doodle to capture it on paper.*

Inspiration #2: *Our mission statement sounds like it was written by a stranger. What happened to the excitement we feel when we tell our friends about what we do?*

Inspiration #3: *Get rid of at least half of the items on our web site and redo the home page to say less and carry more impact.*

BE-Checklist (Simplicity)

- ☐ It works exceptionally well.
- ☐ Nothing feels cluttered or overdone.
- ☐ It is transparent and easily communicated.

Inspiration #1: *Have a reward ceremony once a month for the employee who has come up with the best doodle to capture our vision. Place a copy of that doodle on a prominent wall of our office. Maybe award the winner with a tee shirt with the doodle printed on it?*

Inspiration #2: *Assemble a team of five or six of our staff. Together let us read the mission statement slowly and name any word or phrase that sounds like jargon or is overly complicated. Then let us come up with alternative words to plug into the statement. Then read through it again and add a few elements to evoke goose bumps.*

Inspiration #3: *Let's start with the home page. What can we do to make it feel to the visitor like they have really come home? Can we make it more comfortable? Perhaps a sofa with someone reading our vision with a smile on her face? That's not quite it, but I think if I come to Fran and Tom with this start, they can take it the next step.*

The participant next looks at the checklist in the middle of the sheet. Taking each of the inspiration items, in turn, an assessment is made of how well that item meets the three criteria. Based on that assessment, the item is rewritten in the corresponding space below in slightly more detail.

This last exercise begins the transition back from BE to me. There is no need to abandon the BE-value. It is a resource to be drawn on as often as one likes. Sonya, for example, can draw on Simplicity in other work or life situations as she discovers them becoming overly complicated. Once having played the role of a BE-value, that value is more easily accessed. Returning to it often, that value reshapes one's sense of self in delightful and enlightening ways. One returns, in a real sense, to a different me.

Step 5. Reality Check

As the final step in BE-value explorations, the Reflection/Discussion Guide is used. It consists of two near-identical sets of thought questions. The Reflection Guide is for individual problem-solvers; the Discussion Guide for teams.

The Guide encourages individuals and teams to explore their inspirations through the lenses of these three probes:

1. How can I get started with this?
2. What or who might get in the way of success?
3. How might I use goodness, playfulness, justice, simplicity, and the other BE-values to overcome this resistance?

When a team is working on the same challenge, the members now come together to share their inspirations and agree on next steps. They take turns announcing their BE-value and reading one of their items. As feedback, the other members are encouraged to return to their BE-value role and react to the item from that perspective. For example, as Sonya is reading and briefly describing her second inspiration, Fred-as-Effortlessness listens for ways to infuse that value into Sonya's action item. Susan-as-Completion listens and provides her unique form of feedback. After absorbing this rich feedback, Sonya offers a revised set of steps for moving forward. The next team member then offers an item for exploration.

When all the items have been presented, the team decides on which three inspirations to consider now in more detail. They can vote on these or simply reach consensus through a short round of discussion. The Discussion Guide is then used to explore the realities of each of the three selected inspirations.

As with Step 1 (Zeroing-In), it is ideal to make use of a computer projection system. One person servers as both the facilitator and recorder and is also free to offer input. The trick again is to encourage input from all the participants and still synthesize this feedback and reach consensus in a reasonably short period of time. An experienced facilitator should have no problem in moving a group through this step in around 10-15 minutes. It is a valuable process in its own right as it gets the participants sharing the challenges they see in implementing new ideas in their work or play space.

If appropriate and time permits, the team might compiles a plan of action reflecting the best of what they have learned from each other. In many cases, the team will need the approval and participation of others before moving forward with such a plan. I strongly suggest that they bring their BE-value spirit into play when making their presentations to these stakeholders.

When a group of individuals are working on separate challenges in the same design workshop, a slightly different procedure for sharing can be followed. Taking turns, each presenter will first introduce their challenge statement and offer a small bit of background on why they selected their particular BE-value for tackling it. They will then pick one of their inspirations and use the three questions in the Reflection Guide to briefly consider the realities of implementation. A brief round of feedback then allows each of the other participants to offer reactions to the presentation (ideally speaking with BE-value perspectives). As time permits, each participant may only present one inspiration or may have the opportunity to explore two or three inspirations with the group.

When working alone, one first fills out the Reflection Guide. Then, one can simulate the group feedback process playing multiple roles. As an example, let's say that I have challenged myself to be more centered in my morning hikes. Sitting at my desk, I chose Aliveness as my BE-value for inspiration. I came up with three inspired action items: (1) Stand taller as I walk and feel my shoulders and head reaching upward toward the sky; (2) Add a hop-and-skip rhythm to my walk—not too extreme; and (3) Smile as much as possible without appearing to be the village idiot. I now invite feedback from Barry-as-Wholeness and then from Barry-as-Perfection. I could have chosen any of the other BE-values as well. From Wholeness, I am invited to "melt into" the natural landscape as I walk. From Perfection, I am encouraged to modify my hop-skip gait and image that each step I take is a perfect step.

Concluding Note

Over the years, I have studied and participated in a wide variety of individual and group creativity processes. They are, almost without exception, designed to take one out of one's "normal" way of thinking and invite some form of mental excursion. To the extent that they succeed in shifting consciousness, they do lead to new thoughts and insights. However, the process invariably is artificial.

The use of BE-values is more authentic in the following sense. Everyone has the innate ability to have a peak experience. Some know this, others do not. When peaking, we bring out the best of who we are. Some know how to draw on this potential, others do not. The five-step process introduced above draws on our natural ability to be creative and spiritually alive.

Try it. You'll like it.

6

BE-Value Exploration Guide

This guide will prove useful in tackling virtually any situation in which a person or people are getting in the way of their own excellence (operating at less than peak) and choose to elevate and illuminate their behaviors. A five-step process (BE-value exploration) is offered as a personal or team resource for addressing such challenges.

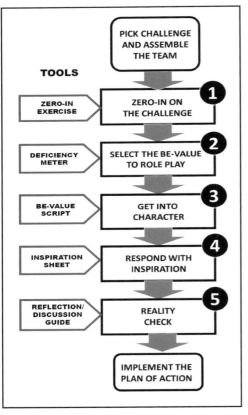

Step 1. The initial statement of the challenge is reviewed through a series of "Why?" and "What?" questions. The aim is to start with a challenge that is closer to the root of the issue at hand.

Step 2. The Deficiency Meter is used to assess inadequacies in the current situation. A BE-value is pinpointed that will be used to fill-in a gap and immediately improve the situation.

Step 3. A one-page script with associated cues are used to grow into the BE-value identify. The aim is to take off one's thinking cap and induce a mild yet potent peak experience and the wisdom that accompanies that experience.

Step 4. Ideas are generated from that BE-value perspective and recorded on an Inspiration Sheet. These ideas are then refined using design criteria associated with the BE-value.

Step 5. A reality check is performed using either the Reflection Guide (individual) or the Discussion Guide (team). The resulting discoveries should be shared with those who potentially will be impacted, as well as trusted friends and peers.

On the following pages, detailed instructions are provided for moving through the process. Solo explorers should skip the items provided in boxes. These are directed to teams tackling a challenge together—to encourage sharing and consensus building. A pair of resource sheets associated with each BE-value is provided in Part 3. A single-page Be-value script consists of (a) five intimations to help identify with the specific BE-value; (b) a short reading to use to embody the spirit of the BE-value; and (c) a set of three core behaviors associated with that BE-value. An Inspiration Sheet for that BE-values is then used to record ideas and test them against three design criteria linked with the value.

Instructions for BE-Value Explorations

Teams: Each member of the team should have his or her own copy of these instructions. Many of the activities will be done as individuals. Proceed as individuals through the first two items.

1. Find a comfortable place to sit. If you can be near a window with a relaxing view, that would be ideal. Have a notepad and pen or pencil with you so you can doodle or write down interesting thoughts that pop into your head. (If you are effortless with a computer or other electronic device, that will also work.)

2. Expect to spend an hour (individual) or two (team). The more relaxed you can be (without drifting into a daydream) the better. Take a few deep breaths every so often (starting right now) to find your center. It also helps to be optimistic that you will come up with some really interesting ideas before you are finished. (As you accumulate experiences with the process, being optimistic will come automatically. It really does work.)

Step One. Zero-In on the Challenge

3. The hardest step in the process comes first. (It's not really that hard, it just forces you to be a bit analytical before getting on to the fun stuff.) Using a blank copy of the **Zero-In Exercise** provided at the end of this section, write down your challenge statement. Begin with a "Why?" question about your motives for tackling this particular challenge, then enter your response.

Teams: Action items 3 through 5 are done together. Use an easel with chart paper, a wall board, or a computer projection system to record progress. Pick a volunteer to serve as recorder. Anyone may pose the "Why?" or "What?" question to address. Multiple members of the team may offer responses that the recorder captures for everyone to see.

4. Looking at that answer, ask yourself a "What?" question to clarify what you just wrote. (It could be a question about the meaning of word or phrase that pops out as you read that begs to be stated differently. It could be a question about what happens if you take the next step and break free of current behaviors.) Write down your response.

5. Then ask and respond to a final "Why?" question. Based on the three responses, but particularly the final one, compose a new challenge statement and compare it with the original version. You should not only see how it is an improvement (gets closer to the root issues preventing excellence), but you also should begin to sense that some interesting

solutions are bubbling up. (If something interesting immediate comes to mind, write it down so you don't worry about losing it.)

Teams: Action items 6 through 14 are performed individually using the same updated challenge statement.

Step Two. Select the BE-Value to Role Play

6. Now is the time to choose the BE-value that will be your ally during the exploration. Get a copy of the **Deficiency Meter (ME)** that appears at the end of this section (for team members, use the **Deficiency Meter (WE)**).   Write down (or key in) your new challenge statement on the top. Then take your time and rate the current against each of the 14 potential shortfalls (deficiencies). (Be tough on yourself. If you have to decide, say, between a rating of 1 or 2, pick 2.)

7. Considering your 14 responses and the BE-values associated with them, select one of the BE-values with the *highest* rating (the most deficiency). (If there are a few with the same rating, they likely will reflect a common theme about the situation.   Pick the one that best seems to capture the spirit of them all.)

   OPTION. For a more in depth process for selecting the BE-value, use the Eupsychian Assessment tool that appears in Appendix A. You will need several more minutes if you use this expanded option. Note that the Assessment tool is based on positive criteria rather than deficiencies. So you will want to choose a BE-value with the *lowest* subtotal rather than the highest rating.

8. Go to the Resource Sheets and get a copy of the two-page set for the BE-value you selected (BE-Value Script and Inspiration Sheet).

9. Using the Inspiration Sheet (the second page), write (or key in) the revised challenge statement. Then put the sheet away for now.

Step Three. Get into Character

10. You are now ready to remove your thinking cap and embody the spirit of the BE-value. Use the **BE-Value Script**. To get into the mood, read through the set of five intimations. Stop at each and make a feeling connection between the item and the BE-value. (How does "a warm bed on a chilly night" afford you a taste of Perfection?). See if you can come up with one or a few additional examples of the BE-value.

11. Go to the reading. Read each paragraph slowly. Pretend that it is you speaking these words out into the world. Be convincing so that if there were listeners, they would believe you mean what you are saying. If you get stuck with (or have problems accepting) a

particular statement, see if you can temporarily suspend judgment. (Remember that this is not you speaking, it is you-as-that-BE-value that is doing the speaking.)

12. When you have completed the reading, consider the core behaviors on the bottom of the page. Feeling yourself as the BE-value, do these behaviors appear consistent with your spirit? Take a few minutes to imagine acting through these behaviors.

Step Four. Respond with Inspiration

13. Return to the **Inspiration Sheet**. Read the challenge statement. Now, from the perspective of the BE-value, write down one imaginative idea for tackling it. Don't write too much, just enough so you won't lose the spark behind the idea. (If you get involved with the writing, you will likely lose the potency of your BE-value experience.) Get centered again in the feeling of the BE-value, look at the challenge statement, and discover another idea for elevating the situation. Write it down. (You can stop now, or if you are on a roll, go for one more idea.)

14. Take a few deep breaths. Take each of your ideas, in turn, and consider how well they meet the three items on the BE-checklist. If not, figure out how to modify the idea so it gets all three check marks. (Even if it passes all three tests, you still might want to make some changes to really capture the spirit behind each of these three design criteria.) Write down the revised version of each idea.

Step Five. Share Discoveries.

15. Get a copy of the **Reflection Guide**. Imagine when, where, and how you can start implementing the idea or ideas. (If you are doing a solo exploration in a room with others who are each working on their own challenge, it is valuable to pair up and take a few minutes to share what you have each learned.)

Teams: Take turns introducing one of your three ideas. Identify the BE-value you were using for inspiration. Team members then offer their reactions to it and perhaps suggest modifications. (They are encouraged to draw on the spirit of their BE-value as they respond.)

After all the ideas have been shared, decide together on three ideas to move forward as a team. Take out the **Discussion Guide** and answer the questions together for each idea. As a final step, the team may choose to combine the ideas into an action plan; or save this step for a later time when other key stakeholders might also be engaged in the planning process.

---

16. Act. (It is useful to have the BE-value walk alongside you as a cheerleader or guide. This will help you draw from its spirit and stay centered as you meet the challenge. Use the Be-Value Script to refresh your spirit.)

Zero-In Exercise

1. What is the challenge (problem, opportunity, design) that we want to address creatively?

> **CHALLENGE AS PRESENTED**:

2. Pick one of these four WHY questions (mark the box with an X). Ask this question about the challenge above. Write your answer in the space provided.

   - ☐ Why is the current situation the way it is?
   - ☐ Why is it worth trying to make a change?
   - ☐ Why isn't it being changed already?
   - ☐ Why is change possible?

> **RESPONSE TO WHY QUESTION**:

3. Now pick one of these four WHAT questions (mark the box with an X). Ask this question about the challenge above. Write your answer in the space provided.

   - ☐ What is interesting about this response?
   - ☐ What change might make a real difference?
   - ☐ What would happen if changes were made?
   - ☐ What has to be given up for changes to happen?

> **RESPONSE TO WHAT QUESTION**:

4. Ask another WHY question (mark the box with an X). Ask this question about the response above. Write your answer in the space provided.

   - ☐ Why is the current situation the way it is?
   - ☐ Why is it worth trying to make a change?
   - ☐ Why isn't it being changed already?
   - ☐ Why is change possible?

> **RESPONSE TO WHY QUESTION**:

5. Now re-write your challenge statement to reflect your best thinking in the above response:

> **RE-STATED CHALLENGE**:

Is it clear why the revised statement will kick-off a richer and more productive exploration?

BKIBEL 2014

Deficiency Meter (ME)

What is the challenge (problem, opportunity, design) that I want to address creatively?

CHALLENGE:

INSTRUCTIONS: RATE each of the 14 deficiencies as they relate to the challenge using this rating scale:

0   No. This is not a problem with our challenge.
1   A bit. This is true to a limited extent.
2   Yes. This is true most or all of the time.
3   Absolutely! This is a truly bad situation that has got to be fixed.

DEFICIENCY TO ADDRESS	RATING		BE-VALUE
Is my success overly dependent on the actions of others?		>	SELF-SUFFICIENCY
Is my viewpoint too fixed and limiting?		>	TRUTHFULNESS
Have I become too weighted down and joyless?		>	PLAYFULNESS
Am I feeling stressed and overloaded?		>	EFFORTLESSNESS
Is there too much sameness and predictability to my approach?		>	UNIQUENESS
Am I acting in ways that are harmful or hurtful?		>	GOODNESS
Does the space I am creating fail to grab and hold attention?		>	BEAUTY
Have things become overly complicated and cluttered?		>	SIMPLICITY
Is the situation one-dimensional?		>	RICHNESS
Is there an absence of positive energy and excitement?		>	ALIVENESS
Am I contributing to an uneven and unfair playing field?		>	JUSTICE
Does it feel like something important is missing?		>	COMPLETION
Are results uninspired and is the potential unrealized?		>	PERFECTION
Is my mindset divisive and fragmented?		>	WHOLENESS

Based on these ratings, which BE-value will I draw on for inspiration?

What will be gained by injecting more of the spirit of this BE-value into the situation?

Deficiency Meter (WE)

What is the challenge (problem, opportunity, design) that we want to address creatively?

CHALLENGE:

INSTRUCTIONS: RATE each of the 14 deficiencies as they relate to the challenge using this rating scale:

0   No. This is not a problem with our challenge.
1   A bit. This is true to a limited extent.
2   Yes. This is true most or all of the time.
3   Absolutely! This is a truly bad situation that has got to be fixed.

DEFICIENCY TO ADDRESS	RATING		BE-VALUE
Is our success overly dependent on the actions of outsiders?		>	SELF-SUFFICIENCY
Is our viewpoint too fixed and limiting?		>	TRUTHFULNESS
Have we become too weighted down and joyless?		>	PLAYFULNESS
Are we feeling stressed and overloaded?		>	EFFORTLESSNESS
Is there too much sameness and predictability to our approach?		>	UNIQUENESS
Are we acting in ways that are harmful or hurtful?		>	GOODNESS
Does the space we are creating fail to grab and hold attention?		>	BEAUTY
Have things become overly complicated and cluttered?		>	SIMPLICITY
Is the situation one-dimensional?		>	RICHNESS
Is there an absence of positive energy and excitement?		>	ALIVENESS
Are we contributing to an uneven and unfair playing field?		>	JUSTICE
Does it feel like something important is missing?		>	COMPLETION
Are results uninspired and is the potential unrealized?		>	PERFECTION
Is our mindset divisive and fragmented?		>	WHOLENESS

Based on these ratings, which BE-value will I draw on for inspiration?

What will be gained by injecting more of the spirit of this BE-value into the situation?

Reflection/Discussion Guide

REFLECTION: The following set of probes is suggested for use when you are **working alone** to explore a challenge. Use it to reflect on each of the action items you would like to move forward.

INSPIRATION #1:

How can I get started with this?

What or who might get in the way of success?

How might I use goodness, playfulness, justice, simplicity, and the other BE-values to overcome this resistance?

INSPIRATION #2:

How can I get started with this?

What or who might get in the way of success?

How might I use goodness, playfulness, justice, simplicity, and the other BE-values to overcome this resistance?

INSPIRATION #3:

How can I get started with this?

What or who might get in the way of success?

How might I use goodness, playfulness, justice, simplicity, and the other BE-values to overcome this resistance?

TEAMS USE THE DISCUSSION GUIDE ON THE NEXT PAGE...

BKIBEL 2014

Reflection/Discussion Guide

DISCUSSION: The following set of probes is suggested for use when you are **working as a team** to explore a challenge. First decide which three inspirations you want to move forward with. Then use these probes to reflect on each. Have someone serve as the recorder.

INSPIRATION #1:

How can we get started with this?

What or who might get in the way of success?

How might we use goodness, playfulness, justice, simplicity, and the other BE-values to overcome this resistance?

INSPIRATION #2:

How can we get started with this?

What or who might get in the way of success?

How might we use goodness, playfulness, justice, simplicity, and the other BE-values to overcome this resistance?

INSPIRATION #3:

How can we get started with this?

What or who might get in the way of success?

How might we use goodness, playfulness, justice, simplicity, and the other BE-values to overcome this resistance?

PART 3

RESOURCE SHEETS

A pair of resources is provided for each of the 14 BE-values: a BE-value Script and an associated Inspiration Sheet. They are essential elements of BE-value explorations (Steps Three and Four). The scripts can also be used on their own for self-study and spiritual growth.

Two additional resources are available for deeper explorations:

The Eupsychian Assessment Tool is provided as Appendix A. You will find this tool useful for in-depth assessments of most situations in which personal or group behaviors are getting in the way of excellence (as defined by peak experiences). Note that this tool differs from the Deficiency Meter in using positive criteria rather than gaps in value.

In Appendix B, a mandala is provided for each BE-value. As an extension of Step Three (Get into Character), select the mandala associated with the BE-value being explored and spend a few minutes centering with it. As with the scripts, the mandalas can be used on their own as meditation tools for self-study and spiritual growth.

BE-VALUE	PAGES	BE-VALUE	PAGES
Self-Sufficiency	53-54	Simplicity	67-68
Truthfulness	55-56	Richness	69-70
Playfulness	57-58	Aliveness	71-72
Effortlessness	59-60	Justice	73-74
Uniqueness	61-62	Completion	75-76
Goodness	63-64	Perfection	77-78
Beauty	65-66	Wholeness	79-80

BE Self-Sufficiency

INTIMATIONS: What does this feel like?

- ❖ Sewing one's own clothes.
- ❖ Growing one's own food.
- ❖ Engaging in sustainable activities (permaculture, water harvesting, etc.).
- ❖ Enjoying one's own company.
- ❖ Walking in time to one's own drummer.
- ❖ Other: _____

READING: On Being Self-Sufficiency

I am the spirit of Self Sufficiency. I am centered and spacious. Here, at the center, time passes by me at a surprisingly slow yet comfortable pace. There is ample opportunity to enjoy the fullness of myself, everyone, and everything. I do not discount the need for others. They add richness to my life and make things possible that I could never do alone. However, I am careful to afford them the same spaciousness as I enjoy, so that they too may be self-sufficient.

There is a strange mental geometry in play. I am situated at the very center of the universe. But, of course, so is everybody else. It is everywhere center, nowhere periphery. A lot of wise people across the ages have reported this to be so during moments of heightened self-awareness and clarity. Like Alice in Wonderland, as fast as you run, you always remain in the same place: at the center—simply Present. .

I am the spirit of Self Sufficiency. I do not seek approval. I approve of myself. There is no need to look elsewhere for proof or validation of my nature. I am creative, loving, and giving. I am grateful to be alive. I expand out from my physical state and view who I am with wisdom and spaciousness, humility and patience. The physical body is my temple. I take care of it. My mind is energy. I regulate it. My soul is infinite. I represent it.

Never mind which part I have to play, I always strive to act it well, so that my role can and support and enlighten others. I do my best and so I feel good about myself. I can only control so much. With faith and trust, I let the rest follow as it may.

CORE BEHAVIORS (Self-Sufficiency)

- ☐ I operate at my very best.
- ☐ I encourage others to operate at their very best.
- ☐ I strive for honesty and authenticity at all times.

INSPIRATION SHEET
BE-Value: **SELF-SUFFICIENCY**

Challenge:

Inspiration #1:

Inspiration #2:

Inspiration #3:

BE-Checklist (Self-Sufficiency)

- ☐ I/we are operating at or near are very best.
- ☐ Others are being encouraged to operate at or near their very best.
- ☐ A spirit of honesty and authenticity is apparent at all or most times.

Inspiration #1:

Inspiration #2:

Inspiration #3:

BE Truthfulness

- ❖ A march for civil rights.
- ❖ Walking away from an unhealthy situation.
- ❖ Learning from and not repeating the mistakes of the past.
- ❖ Choosing the high road.
- ❖ Listening with an open heart.
- ❖ Other: _____

READING: On Being Truthfulness

I am the spirit of Truthfulness. I center and relax, take the leap and *faith* passed my own cleverness and essential ignorance. With a silent and receptive mind, I accept without defending, delight without second-guessing, and draw on an unexplainable source of wisdom to catalyze my potential for brilliance. Inspiration invariably follows.

A different kind of *knowing* is at work. It is not fact and memory that dominate. Instead there is the sensation of having an unadulterated view of reality, beyond words, and being okay with that. I am alert to the clues, to the odd synchronicities, to sudden twists of fate. They are *always* there in direct response to my reaching outward with a question or a challenge to this grand and reliable source of wisdom. This wisdom extends deeper and wider than what logic can reproduce or rationally digest. It is up to me how much of the Immeasurable becomes real for me. Accessing this wisdom involves quieting the mind, the application of the heart, and the creative synthesis of reason and feeling.

These encounters are not lined up to be mastered in some predetermined order, as some new body of knowledge. They have no time-space association with each other, but each encounter guarantees an association with reality that always appears *new* each time it is encountered. It lacks density, for everything in it permeates everything else. It lacks duration: if I cling to it, it vanishes. It cannot be surveyed; if I try to survey it, it is lost. It does not stand outside me, it touches my very ground of being. I do not process this experience, analytically and sequentially. I stand back and view the whole, discern what matters and what does not, and weigh the meaning and depth of things.

CORE BEHAVIORS (Truthfulness)

- ☐ I am receptive to clues and insights beyond the five senses.
- ☐ I resist fixed, know-it-all points of view.
- ☐ I maintain integrity and honesty no matter what.

INSPIRATION SHEET
BE-Value: **TRUTHFULNESS**

Challenge:

Inspiration #1:

Inspiration #2:

Inspiration #3:

BE-Checklist (Truthfulness)

- ☐ There is openness to clues and insights beyond the five senses.
- ☐ Fixed, know-it-all points of view are discouraged.
- ☐ Integrity and honesty are maintained no matter what.

Inspiration #1:

Inspiration #2:

Inspiration #3:

BE Playfulness

INTIMATIONS: What does this feel like?

- ❖ Ticking a young child.
- ❖ A kitten with a spool of yarn.
- ❖ A costume party.
- ❖ Hunting for Easter eggs.
- ❖ An outing to the zoo or to the beach.
- ❖ Other: _____

READING: On Being Playfulness

I am the spirit of Playfulness. You can't miss me in the room or on the street. I have a grin on my face that seems a bit too large and inappropriate for the situation. I am not smiling at the situation itself. I am smiling at the fact that the situation exists at all—that we are somehow rotating around the sun and through the cosmos, a speck in the universe, and yet taking ourselves so, so serious. If you haven't discovered this yet, I'll tell it to you now: saints and creative individuals in all fields are still kids. They have to be.

We think too much. Thoughts are heavy. They tend to weight us down and keep us earth-bound. Genuine smiles achieve the opposite result: we find ourselves levitating. Whenever I catch myself becoming too serious, overly solemn, too clever for my own good, too rigid in defending a position, I *become* a smile. I start at the mouth and then fill my entire mind-body with that smile. And I instantly feel lighter.

Taking a serious approach to serious problems just adds unnecessary cleverness to the drama. This truly doesn't get me or others very far toward a unique and exciting solution, particularly to one that adds exuberance to the universe. For inspiration, whether the challenge is professional or personal, I reflect on what might bring joy into play.

I am the spirit of Playfulness. I make fun of myself and of situations. I never make fun *at* someone else's expense. That type of humor is mean-spirited and does not elevate the situation. I aim for levity: to rise up beyond fears and worries. As the saying goes, angels can fly because they know how to take themselves lightly.

CORE BEHAVIORS (Playfulness)

☐ An innocent and childlike quality sets my mood.

☐ I leave ample room to try new things.

☐ I make conscious efforts to have fun in ways that invite others to join in.

INSPIRATION SHEET
BE-Value: **PLAYFULNESS**

Challenge:

Inspiration #1:

Inspiration #2:

Inspiration #3:

BE-Checklist (Playfulness)

☐ An innocent and childlike quality sets the mood.

☐ There is ample room to try new things.

☐ Conscious efforts are made to have fun in ways that invite others to join in.

Inspiration #1:

Inspiration #2:

Inspiration #3:

BE Effortlessness

INTIMATIONS: What does this feel like?

- ❖ A professional basketball player dunking the ball; an end leaping up to catch a football.
- ❖ A ballet dancer circling across the stage.
- ❖ Preparing a dinner that you have done dozens of times.
- ❖ A lion in the wild stalking its prey.
- ❖ Falling asleep as one's eyes close by themselves.
- ❖ Other: _____

READING: On Being Effortlessness

I am the spirit of Effortlessness. I live my life as if *I am not*. The less I am, the more healthy I am, the more weightless I am, the more cloudlike I am, the more I am free. A white cloud hovers in the sky, timeless because there is no future and no mind to it. No resistance, no fight, nothing to be achieved, nothing to be lost. Just drifting, and by and by being merged. Drifting, not moving to a point—just drifting wherever the winds lead it.

I relax my hold on pictures of how things "ought" to be, and learn to make peace with things as they *are*. I do this moment by moment, here and now, responding with an open heart and mind to the changes that occur. Whatever the tasks, I do them with ease, in mindfulness. My aim is to engage in them, rather than to get them over with. When I walk up a steep slope, I don't think about the end, I just take the next step. I don't create any fight inside my head. I simply do. And, in this way, I am beyond my head, beyond my ego's pull.

Living without effort to get somewhere else, much more immediately becomes possible. I am more open, less closed, more vulnerable, more receptive. Life passes through me. It comes and goes, and I allow it. When I am empty, when just a vacuum exists, I am primed to enter into each situation with freshness and novelty. I travel light, I live light. I am in rhythm with life's conditions. Lennon and McCartney surely caught the spirit when they wrote: Let it be, let it be, let it be, let it be. There will be an answer, let it be." Out of the silence, I hear what I am capable of understanding and assessing based on my unique set of skills, talents, and experiences. I am enriched by this ability and I enrich others through what I hear, absorb, and speak or act out. I am "in the zone." I am at my best. I am the spirit of Effortlessness.

CORE BEHAVIORS (Effortlessness)

- ☐ If anything appears complicated, I simplify it.

- ☐ If anything feels stressful, I take a deep breath and relax.

- ☐ I strive for natural ease and grace even amid the more hectic surface activities.

INSPIRATION SHEET
BE-Value: **EFFORTLESSNESS**

Challenge:

Inspiration #1:

Inspiration #2:

Inspiration #3:

BE-Checklist (Effortlessness)

☐ Nothing appears complicated.

☐ Nothing feels stressful.

☐ A natural ease and grace underlies the more hectic surface activities.

Inspiration #1:

Inspiration #2:

Inspiration #3:

BE Uniqueness

INTIMATIONS: What does this feel like?

- ❖ A jazz musician or singer whose sound is immediately recognized.
- ❖ A painter employing an original style or medium.
- ❖ The special qualities of one's child or spouse.
- ❖ A culture experienced that is unlike one's own.
- ❖ The Grand Canyon.
- ❖ Other: _____

READING: On Being Uniqueness

I am the spirit of Uniqueness. I have learned that to really see something as it truly is, I have to look at it with the innocent eyes of a child—as though I have never seen anything like it before. I don't project images or experiences with similar things on the current object or person or scene of attention. With an open mind, I let that object, person, or scene reveal itself in its own terms. I hold up my hand, palm facing me. This hand of mine has never has looked *exactly* like this before. It has never stopped changing: getting a bit older, but also renewing itself. No two set of fingerprints are precisely like mine; even more so for this skin-glove of mine. The longer I look at my hand, the more I am presented with interesting lines and other unique details.

I am the spirit of Uniqueness. I have penetrated passed all the imagery and conclusions I have previously drawn about myself and have discovered a totally mysterious and far more interesting person right here. I have no idea *exactly* who I am or even *what* I am. I am more space than object, more spirit than matter, more godlike than animal. There has never been anyone exactly like me ever before. Isn't it amazing that with more than 7 billion people in the world, each and every one of us remains extraordinarily unique? Here we all are, each following unique life paths and adding to the extraordinary diversity of the world.

What I have to say has never been said exactly this way before. What I have to contribute comes from someone who has never before existed in this world in precisely this way. I do not aim to be different... I simply am different. I am here to express this difference through my actions and in my relationships. I am also here to encourage the uniqueness in others to flourish. Let us all surprise and delight each other in the best of all possible ways.

CORE BEHAVIORS (Uniqueness)

☐ I try not to repeat myself.

☐ I avoid what is typical and expected.

☐ I take the risk of being different.

INSPIRATION SHEET
BE-Value: UNIQUENESS

Challenge:

Inspiration #1:

Inspiration #2:

Inspiration #3:

BE-Checklist (Uniqueness)

- ☐ This is the first of its kind in at least one important way.
- ☐ It stands out from what is typical and expected.
- ☐ Its added value justifies the risk of being different.

Inspiration #1:

Inspiration #2:

Inspiration #3:

BE Goodness

- ❖ The Good Samaritan.
- ❖ A community rallying together after a natural disaster.
- ❖ A child giving a last piece of candy to someone who needs it more.
- ❖ Spontaneous acts of kindness.
- ❖ Helping someone cross the street.
- ❖ Other: _____

READING: On Being Goodness

I am the spirit of Goodness. I am conscientious in regard to the feelings of others, I am ready to serve them, to please them, to forgive them, and—where unfortunately necessary—to tolerate them. My goodness is not something which I acquired or struggle to find; it springs up whenever I lead with my heart. It is not something I create; it is already here. It is what I am, not what I become.

I use *heart* words, not mind words. As I speak from my heart, I find myself saying surprising and often illuminating things. As I listen in a heart-centered way, I tend to hear what lies *behind* the surface. I simply let go of "I'm right!" and present my deepest self, my deepest feelings, my deepest awareness, and then *see* what happens. I enjoy the feeling of gentle helpfulness that rises up spontaneously and translates to actions that are appreciated by those I reach.

The end and the sum total of my life, of everything I have learned and developed, is to be a good person and to do good for others. Every good quality that I express in thought and action is meant to yield the hidden nectar of goodness; and does so, when my inner perception is deep enough. I perform helpful and often loving actions because they *feel* good as well as to produce good results. I find my happiness increases as I increase my kindness. And as I practice kindness towards others, I practice kindness toward myself. When I am kind to myself, I immediately feel a response. There is an essence, a power, a substance, a Light in my physical body that is kindled. I am turning up the power, flaming the flame, letting in the Light. I give from my center—and I am replenished.

CORE BEHAVIORS (Goodness)

- ☐ I intend for all my relationships and interactions to be positive and kind.
- ☐ I try always to be helpful.
- ☐ I aim to raise consciousness and spirit.

INSPIRATION SHEET
BE-Value: **GOODNESS**

Challenge:

Inspiration #1:

Inspiration #2:

Inspiration #3:

BE-Checklist (Goodness)

☐ Positive relationships and interactions are encouraged.

☐ Positive relationships and interactions are rewarded.

☐ Attention is drawn to humanity when at its best.

Inspiration #1:

Inspiration #2:

Inspiration #3:

BE Beauty

INTIMATIONS: What does this feel like?

- ❖ A sunset.
- ❖ A rainbow.
- ❖ A bouquet of freshly cut flowers.
- ❖ A South Seas black pearl.
- ❖ A gentle spirit.
- ❖ Other: _____

READING: On Being Beauty

I am the spirit of Beauty. I am fully *present*. I experience the moment in an innocent, childlike state of wonder. I interface in the moment with whatever is before me. I enjoy each moment with its pure, natural, exciting, amazing, pulsating forms. I give those things I instinctively don't like the same close attention as those I enjoy, and I am always pleasantly surprised at what happens. I do it, not for any ethical or even great cosmic reason, but because I know that everything is wonder-filled and available to delight.

I have eyes of wonder. "Eyes of wonder" are eyes of innocence, eyes not jaded and obscured by preconceptions and notions. When I see a waterfall, or a rainbow, or a stormy sea, or a newborn baby, I am overwhelmed with feelings of reverence and wonder. Every single object or person on which my eyes fall and hold is remarkable. The longer I remain fixed on that object or person, the more it draws me into its forms and essence. The edges appear more round or more sharply defined. The components seem more intricately designed, each contributing to the integrity of the whole.

Moments of delight are not far off and do not require voyages around the world or to the beach or mountains. They are at my fingertips at all times, because I stop and pay attention to the beauty that dances around me. I do not measure and shrink and try to define or explain what makes everything and everyone so beautiful. I simply keep my eyes open and experience the wonder of it all. I am overwhelmed with feelings of deep appreciation. All "things" pass away, but the inner beauty that I see with wonder, I know endures—it is timeless.

CORE BEHAVIORS (Beauty)

☐ I appreciate the endless wonders and beauty in the world.

☐ I look for and discover the inner beauty in whatever I behold.

☐ I acknowledge my own inner beauty and aim to let it shine outward.

INSPIRATION SHEET
BE-Value: **BEAUTY**

Challenge:

Inspiration #1:

Inspiration #2:

Inspiration #3:

BE-Checklist (Beauty)

☐ There is rich appeal to the senses.

☐ It has the "Wow!" factor.

☐ It draws people to it.

Inspiration #1:

Inspiration #2:

Inspiration #3:

BE Simplicity

INTIMATIONS: What does this feel like?

- ❖ A picnic of fresh fruit, cheese, bread, and wine.
- ❖ Easy-to-follow instructions for assembling a product.
- ❖ A Zen garden.
- ❖ Modest and comfortable clothing.
- ❖ A love song sung and played on a guitar.
- ❖ Other: _____

READING: On Being Simplicity

I am the spirit of Simplicity. I am true to the moment. When hungry I eat, when tired I sleep. Thoughts do not weight me down. They take up hardly any room at all. My sentences are short. My words have few syllables and are easy to spell. When I look at an object, it looks back at me. There is space in which to relax, and discover what lies below the surface noises.

The ultimate simplicity is expressed in the invitation: "Be here, now." Being in the moment is not something I have to do. It is something I am always doing and cannot cease to do. This moment is where I am, and this moment is all there is. It is what's happening. I do not dwell in the past or invent the future. I am not haunted by a sense that the ways I like to spend my time—sitting under a tree, for instance, or listening quietly to music—are trivial, and somehow wrong. In fact, when I am "unproductive" in these ways, some of my best discoveries occur. This doesn't mean that I won't wear a watch, or follow a schedule, or make plans for tomorrow, but rather that I remain fully attentive to each activity I carry out and do it simply.

I do one thing at a time. When I am drinking tea, I drink tea. When I am reading the paper, I read the paper. This helps to slow the mind and stop time-bound patterns. When I attend, with care, to a single, present activity, I discover a wonderful freedom from thought. In the next sip of tea, the next breath, the next step, no clock time exists, and with each opportunity I take to come fully into the moment, I feel the relief of resting in the Present. I live my live aware there is a vibrant, silent, creative mystery everywhere, ever present, and in everything. I am aware of it and let it enrich me and guide me. I trust the moment to reveal the truth of that moment. I just live simply and allow it to happen.

CORE BEHAVIORS (Simplicity)

☐ I get satisfaction from devising simpler ways to do things.

☐ I aim to remove clutter in my physical world and in my mind.

☐ I strive for clear and transparent communication.

INSPIRATION SHEET
BE-Value: SIMPLICITY

Challenge:

Inspiration #1:

Inspiration #2:

Inspiration #3:

BE-Checklist (Simplicity)

- ☐ It works exceptionally well.
- ☐ Nothing feels cluttered or overdone.
- ☐ It is transparent and easily communicated.

Inspiration #1:

Inspiration #2:

Inspiration #3:

BE Richness

- ❖ Perfectly spiced Asian cuisine.
- ❖ A freshly brewed cup of coffee together with a croissant just out of the oven.
- ❖ The human brain at work.
- ❖ Nature and all its wonders.
- ❖ A lively conversation in which all parties are engaged in discovery.
- ❖ Other: _____

READING: On Being Richness

I am the spirit of Richness. I do not allow any situation to remain one-dimensional. With each additional dimension I add, there is increased potential for deeper experience and fuller enjoyment. I add texture. I add color. I add aroma. I add spice. It is easy to overdo it, of course. Too much of a color or the wrong choice of spice can wreck the harmony and muddle the result. I pride myself on *knowing* what to add next, and how much, to produce greater complexity without sacrificing integrity. I move from whole to whole to whole; resting just long enough to insure the integrity of the current whole before leaping forward to new adventures.

I take risks. I bring elements together that usually are kept apart. My goal is to stimulate imagination and open fresh possibilities for going farther and deeper. Each seeming end point is always a new beginning for me. I may start out to address a specific shortfall that needs correction and find success. Then, as a bonus, I use the solution that has emerged as the launching point for a complementary creative exploration with new ingredients, participants, and objectives. There is no stopping me. I crave symphonies, not fiddle playing.

I employ less reason, more trust; less practicality, more adventure; less prose, more poetry. In short, I am meta-logical. Every step I take says to me: "Go beyond it, much more is hidden beyond." *Beyond* becomes the goal—transcend everything and go beyond. Then life remains an adventure, a continuous discovery of the unknown. The journey is ongoing, endless, flexible, expansive and deepening. The path is ever exciting, ever playful, ever extending.

CORE BEHAVIORS (Richness)

☐ I am always on the lookout for ways to enrich my life.

☐ I am always on the lookout for ways to enrich the lives of others.

☐ I enjoy challenges that make me think "outside the box."

INSPIRATION SHEET
BE-Value: RICHNESS

Challenge:

Inspiration #1:

Inspiration #2:

Inspiration #3:

BE-Checklist (Richness)

- ☐ There is an overflow of possibilities here.
- ☐ It holds appeal for broad and diverse people.
- ☐ The deeper the probe, the more qualities are discovered.

Inspiration #1:

Inspiration #2:

Inspiration #3:

BE Aliveness

INTIMATIONS: What does this feel like?

- ❖ Waking up in the morning and raring to get started with the day.
- ❖ Gazelles leaping across an open field.
- ❖ An active volcano.
- ❖ A butterfly emerging from the chrysalis.
- ❖ An excited audience applauding a wonderful performance.
- ❖ Other: _____

READING: On Being Aliveness

I am the spirit of Aliveness. I listen to the sounds of birds chirping. I smell the bouquet of a rose or of bread turning to toast. I rub my fingers together. I feel my body meeting the chair or sofa. Then, widening my field of awareness beyond my head and body, I encounter something sublime, something beyond mind, beyond nature, and even beyond wonder.

I do not get lost in the mechanics of life, and go dull. I do not go through the motions of living and relating, and forget to celebrate the moment itself and what adventures it holds. Instead I bring curiosity and radical amazement to every life encounter, recognizing and appreciating both finite and infinite dimensions. Consequently, I aim to be immense. Whatever I encounter, from a flower petal to the beehive of life on a street in Manhattan, I meet through the fresh eyes of an immense and infinite being. In response, the immensity of the petal or scene reflects and responds back at me. It presents to me its own aliveness and appears to glow from within. Each of its details now seems perfect in detail and form. I remain alert, and by and by energies are transformed. The finite dims as the infinite is revealed.

I tingle with the excitement of living in the creative moment. I willingly accept my individual responsibilities to stay receptive and attuned to what each moment offers. I feel the mist of grace and experience its powers to invigorate, enrich, and levitate me beyond the gravity forces of the physical world. I grasp the fullness of life's forces as these impinge on me. I permit these forces to reflect back out from my very being, transforming me and everything around me with excitement and new meaning. My soul soars high.

CORE BEHAVIORS (Aliveness)

☐ There is a lot of passion behind everything I do.

☐ I enjoy being spontaneous and surprising others.

☐ When I get excited about something, I throw a lot of energy into it.

INSPIRATION SHEET
BE-Value: **ALIVENESS**

Challenge:

Inspiration #1:

Inspiration #2:

Inspiration #3:

BE-Checklist (Aliveness)

☐ High energy and high performance are evident.

☐ Passion and spontaneity are actively promoted.

☐ Surprise is a valued output.

Inspiration #1:

Inspiration #2:

Inspiration #3:

BE Justice

INTIMATIONS: What does this feel like?

- ❖ Taking action to right a wrong.
- ❖ Allowing all voices to be heard and appreciated.
- ❖ The Special Olympics.
- ❖ Religious freedom.
- ❖ Equal pay for equal work.
- ❖ Other: _____

READING: On Being Justice

I am the spirit of Justice. I aim to do what is right. I do what in my heart of hearts I know is fair and just. This applies to my personal choices and actions. It applies in my interactions with others, as expressed in the golden rule, "Do unto others as you would have them do unto you." It applies in my work ethics and in my role within our collective stewardship of the environment.

Logic and observation tell me that the world is not fair, that only the strong or well-networked survive. Perhaps, I tell myself, I should also join the ranks of the takers and hoarders. However, my inner voice offers a different and stronger message. I am "hard wired" to have integrity. I cannot be truly alive to the moment and still take advantage of another and feel good about it. My integrity does not permit that. I share space rather than compete for dominance of it. I seek win-win solutions rather than "I win, you lose." I exhibit concern and interest instead of hatred or jealousy. I return good for evil, by being compassionate and generous with my time and resources.

I exercise the integrity which comes from seeing things *whole* and acting from wholeness. I aim to erase artificial boundaries that separate rather than unite. I employ both logic and compassion to each new situation, favoring compassion over logic when such choices are required. At a level beyond thought, I know that the soul rules the mind and that the "best" decisions and actions are those that are soul-felt. I am not fooled by clever arguments that lead to more harm than good and further uneven the fields of play.

CORE BEHAVIORS (Justice)

☐   I do not pre-judge persons and ideas.

☐   I do not draw conclusions prematurely.

☐   I view differences as positives to be celebrated and synergized.

INSPIRATION SHEET
BE-Value: **JUSTICE**

Challenge:

Inspiration #1:

Inspiration #2:

Inspiration #3:

BE-Checklist (Justice)

☐ Persons and ideas are not pre-judged.

☐ Conclusions are not drawn prematurely.

☐ Differences are viewed as opportunities to add richness.

Inspiration #1:

Inspiration #2:

Inspiration #3:

BE Completion

INTIMATIONS: What does this feel like?

- ❖ Placing the last piece on a jigsaw puzzle.
- ❖ Putting the final touches on a large renovation project.
- ❖ The end to a wonderful dinner.
- ❖ Proving a theory or a solving a challenging mathematical problem.
- ❖ Dying with dignity and in peace.
- ❖ Other: _____

READING: On Being Completion

I am the spirit of Completion. I have discovered, digested, and integrated within me that last missing ingredient. I am now whole. I am perfect. I am fulfilled. There is something truly satisfying about being fully myself in this way. That final ingredient that had alluded me has worked its alchemy. It has tied loose ends together. It has brought seeming opposites within me into harmony. It has transported me to a state of being I have wanted to attain for so long. And now that I am here, I realize that it is paradoxically everything I thought it would be, yet feels unlike anything I had imagined. It is much more. It brings unexpected joy.

I exist in a serene and elevated state that is both simple and pure. There is an absence of emotional drama. There is an absence of psychological clutter. There is no want, no desire, and no fear. However, I am not a vacuum. I am overflowing with a sense of just-rightness. Yes, this *is* it. I am somehow "home" again. This is where I am always meant to be.

I do not try to manipulate my experiences to channel them in one way versus another. I moderate my inner and outer movements with a single aim in mind: to savor these moments of being home while I am blessed to be here. If I feel a pull or push, I stop and consider how I can address these without leaving home... without losing my center. This requires a fine balancing act of responding to the finite requirements of the moment while maintaining my center.

The itching for new adventure is also an expression of my true nature. I am not immune from the ever-changing universe. Following this period of completion, of respite, it will be a new and improved "me" that ventures forward in response to a new calling. The question which time will answer: Will I lose my center or can I maintain this state of completeness as I strike out again?

CORE BEHAVIORS (Completion)

☐ I always deliver on my commitments in a timely manner.

☐ I make sure that whatever I do meets or exceeds expectations.

☐ I begin each new tasks with a fresh and open outlook.

INSPIRATION SHEET
BE-Value: COMPLETION

Challenge:

Inspiration #1:

Inspiration #2:

Inspiration #3:

BE-Checklist (Completion)

☐ It is working as intended and promised.

☐ Nothing essential appears to have been ignored.

☐ The stage is set for a new and exciting beginning.

Inspiration #1:

Inspiration #2:

Inspiration #3:

BE Perfection

INTIMATIONS: What does this feel like?

- ❖ A bowling ball curving into the pocket and sending all ten pins flying.
- ❖ A newborn infant in her mother's arms.
- ❖ Making a slight adjustment to a crooked painting hanging on the wall.
- ❖ A warm bed on a chilly night.
- ❖ A shoulder and back rub.
- ❖ Other: _____

READING: On Being Perfection

I am the spirit of Perfection. When I act, no matter how small the deed, I resonate with all that is perfect about the world. I have no concern for bottom-line results or end states. And I surely do not embrace my flaws, and accept myself as an "imperfect" being. I take my very next step with focused attention, integrity, and as much brilliance and wholeness as I can bring into play.

It is not uncommon to hear adults complain that when they were children their parents expected them to be "perfect" all the time. As a result, when they hear the term, perfect, they are instinctively defensive. Perfection earns this bad reputation when it is confused with "perfectionism." Perfectionism is a curse and a strain. Perfection is a blessing and a joy. I am not afraid of mistakes. Mistakes are not sins. Mistakes when done with integrity are ways of doing something different, perhaps creatively new. I am not sorry for these mistakes. I am proud of them. I have had the courage to give something of myself.

I resonate with these words of Marianne Williamson: "There is nothing enlightened about shrinking so that other people won't feel insecure around you. We are all meant to shine, as children do... And as we let our own light shine, we unconsciously give other people permission to do the same." I have no interest in being average. I do not measure my life against others. I relentlessly pursue standards of absolute excellence. No half-way measures or relative successes are enough; only absolutes satisfy my soul. Absolute honesty, absolute gentleness, absolute caring, unwearied patience and thoughtfulness in the midst of the push-pulls of home and office and society.

CORE BEHAVIORS (Perfection)

☐   I always give my absolute best effort.

☐   I aim to be inspiring.

☐   I produce results that are dazzling.

INSPIRATION SHEET
BE-Value: PERFECTION

Challenge:

Inspiration #1:

Inspiration #2:

Inspiration #3:

BE-Checklist (Perfection)

- ☐ This is our/my absolute best effort.
- ☐ This is truly inspiring.
- ☐ The overall results are dazzling.

Inspiration #1:

Inspiration #2:

Inspiration #3:

BE Wholeness

INTIMATIONS: What does this feel like?

- ❖ The planet Earth.
- ❖ Humanity.
- ❖ An orchestra.
- ❖ A high-performing sports team.
- ❖ A jazz quartet.
- ❖ Other: _____

READING: On Being Wholeness

I am the spirit of Wholeness. I smile. I am alert to what is happening all around me. My concentration and attention are equally focused on the things I see, on the sounds I hear, on the mood of the space. This activity involves me completely and my thoughts are not drifting off or jumping about. All the objects in my field of vision exist as a single composition. The distinction between foreground and background is scarcely relevant. The background and the foreground are equalized. Every object in my space, me included, as well as the space itself, appear to be one common substance: essence or is-ness. Nothing appears hurried, and yet whatever is unfolding and its speed of advance are perfect. It is all happening just as it should.

I am unusually passive, receptive, humble, and yet overjoyed with wonder. I am truly content just being in contact with life's many mysteries, to listen, to hear, and to be transformed by them. I realize that, as incredible as it seems to the intellect, every event and everything in the universe is somehow in constant contact with every other event and thing, being "fed" by each other and, in turn, feeding back out into the world what has been received.

I am not some isolated creature struggling to survive and prosper among other isolated creatures. I am intimately connected to all men and women within a web. When I act, the web moves. When the web moves, I am moved. Live is not divided. Oneness is felt. Time disappears, space becomes meaningless. I simply *am* and this moment is eternal. I witness the whole time process as just a long extended NOW. I witness the whole of space as just expanded HERE.

CORE BEHAVIORS (Wholeness)

☐ I lead my life as a coherent whole (I am not fragmented).

☐ I relate to the universe as a coherent whole (I celebrate its oneness).

☐ I remain open to life's many mysteries.

INSPIRATION SHEET
BE-Value: **WHOLENESS**

Challenge:

Inspiration #1:

Inspiration #2:

Inspiration #3:

BE-Checklist (Wholeness)

- ☐ It works as, and feels like, a single, well-integrated composition.
- ☐ Each person and component is central; none are peripheral.
- ☐ Each new input (person or component) is easily assimilated.

Inspiration #1:

Inspiration #2:

Inspiration #3:

Appendix A. EUPSYCHIAN ASSESSMENT TOOL

Situation:	
Date:	Completed By:

Instructions: Assess the current situation in terms of each set of three criteria, using the rating scheme to the right to score each criterion. After completing each section, calculate the subtotal and note down any immediate actions you might take or encourage to elevate the situation.

When finished, record and add the 14 subtotals on the last page and divide that sum by 2.1 to obtain your TOTAL SCORE. The ideal is 100. A score of 60 or more is actually quite good. For BE-value explorations, pick a BE-value with the lowest subtotal.

Rating for Current Situation	
Exemplary	5
Fully Met	4
Mostly Met	3
Somewhat Met	2
Barely Met	1
Not Met At All	0

SELF-SUFFICIENCY
RATING

I/we are operating at or near are very best.	
Others are being encouraged to operate at or near their very best.	
A spirit of honesty and authenticity is apparent at all or most times.	
SUBTOTAL (MAX = 15)	

Is my/our success overly dependent on the actions of outsiders? Where to add more Self-Sufficiency?

TRUTHFULNESS
RATING

There is openness to clues and insights beyond the five senses.	
Fixed, know-it-all points of view are discouraged.	
Integrity and honesty are maintained no matter what.	
SUBTOTAL (MAX = 15)	

Is my/our viewpoint too fixed and limiting? Where to add more Truthfulness?

PLAYFULNESS
RATING

An innocent and childlike quality sets the mood.	
There is ample room to try new things.	
Conscious efforts are made to have fun in ways that invite others to join in.	
SUBTOTAL (MAX = 15)	

Have I/we become too weighted down and joyless? Where to add more Playfulness?

EFFORTLESSNESS

RATING

Nothing appears complicated.	
Nothing feels stressful.	
A natural ease and grace underlies the more hectic surface activities.	
SUBTOTAL (MAX = 15)	

Am I/are we feeling stressed and overloaded? Where to add more Effortlessness?

UNIQUENESS

RATING

This is the first of its kind in at least one important way.	
It stands out from what is typical and expected.	
Its added value justifies the risk of being different.	
SUBTOTAL (MAX = 15)	

Is there too much sameness and predictability to my/our approach? Where to add more Uniqueness?

GOODNESS

RATING

Positive relationships and interactions are encouraged.	
Positive relationships and interactions are rewarded.	
Attention is drawn to humanity when at its best.	
SUBTOTAL (MAX = 15)	

Am I/are we acting in ways that are harmful or hurtful? Where to add more Goodness?

BEAUTY

RATING

There is rich appeal to the senses.	
It has the "Wow!" factor.	
It draws people to it.	
SUBTOTAL (MAX = 15)	

Does the space I/we are creating fail to grab and hold attention? Where to add more Beauty?

SIMPLICITY

It works exceptionally well.	
Nothing feels cluttered or overdone.	
It is transparent and easily communicated.	
SUBTOTAL (MAX = 15)	

Have things become overly complicated and cluttered? Where to add more Simplicity?

RICHNESS

RATING

There is an overflow of possibilities here.	
It holds appeal for broad and diverse people.	
The deeper the probe, the more qualities are discovered.	
SUBTOTAL (MAX = 15)	

Is the situation one-dimensional? Where to add more Richness?

ALIVENESS

RATING

High energy and high performance are evident.	
Passion and spontaneity are actively promoted.	
Surprise is a valued output.	
SUBTOTAL (MAX = 15)	

Is there an absence of positive energy and excitement? Where to add more Aliveness?

JUSTICE

RATING

Persons and ideas are not pre-judged.	
Conclusions are not drawn prematurely	
Differences are viewed as opportunities to add richness.	
SUBTOTAL (MAX = 15)	

Am I/are we contributing to an uneven and unfair playing field? Where to add more Justice?

COMPLETION

It is working as intended and promised.	
Nothing essential appears to have been ignored.	
The stage is set for a new and exciting beginning.	
SUBTOTAL (MAX = 15)	

Does it feel like something important is missing? Where to add more Completion?

PERFECTION

RATING

This is our/my absolute best effort.	
This is truly inspiring.	
The overall results are dazzling.	
SUBTOTAL (MAX = 15)	

Are results uninspired and is the potential unrealized? Where to add more Perfection?

WHOLENESS

RATING

It works as, and feels like, a single, well-integrated composition.	
Each person and component is central; none are peripheral.	
Each new input (person or component) is easily assimilated.	
SUBTOTAL (MAX = 15)	

Is my/our mindset divisive and fragmented? Where to add more Wholeness?

Enter the 14 subtotals and add them together (max = 210):

Self-Sufficiency		Goodness		Justice	
Truthfulness		Beauty		Completion	
Playfulness		Simplicity		Perfection	
Effortlessness		Richness		Wholeness	
Uniqueness		Aliveness		**SUM**	

TOTAL SCORE = SUM / 2.1 =	

84

Appendix B
BE-Value Mandalas

For deeper immersion into the spirit of any of the BE-values, a complementary mandala has been created. Each mandala was uniquely developed to bring to life that spirit in shape and color. They were designed by the graphic artist, Toni Arnon, and appear on the following pages, two to a page.

For each mandala, the question from the Deficiency Meter appears in the bottom right corner. In the other three corners are symptoms or behaviors that tend to be associated with that deficiency. The aim of any mandala is to become centered. The four key words in white that surround the mandala were chosen to ease entry into the mandala and movement toward its center. At the very center of the mandala, barely visible, is the word BE.

Here is how I center with a BE-mandala:

> ➤ For around two minutes, I don't think about the specific design challenge. Instead, I just aim to become increasingly comfortable working with the words and graphics on the mandala and the feelings in me that that each positive and negative word generates.

> ➤ I pick the deficiency word or phrase in one of the three corners, feel its meaning, and then slowly move my attention toward the center. As I move inward, I try to convert that feeling of deficiency to the spirit of the BE-value. For example, I make the transition from the feeling of boredom to that of Aliveness. Or the feeling of vulgarity to that of Beauty.

> ➤ I embody the BE-value spirit for as long as I can. When I find myself drifting, I slowly move back out and find another word or phrase at the periphery. I use it to draw back to the center. I continue in this way until time runs out

This centering activity awakens the spirit not only of the target BE-value but also the spirit of the other BE-values as well. While centering with one mandala, it is common to experience wholeness, completeness, perfection, aliveness, self-sufficiency, and the rest of the 14 values.

When others are doing this exercise in the same room, the mind-body changes taking place can easily be observed. There definitely is an energy-shift in the room. One colleague might look over at another, their eyes meet, and both spontaneously start to smile or laugh. Others may join in as the collective expansion of consciousness is experienced.

The aim is to realize the full benefits of this switch from me to BE. Hopefully the lingering effects will light up your day and life. Returning to the mandalas from time to time, either for BE-value explorations or simple spiritual refreshment, is highly recommended. There is a lot of spiritual wisdom packed into these seemingly simple designs.

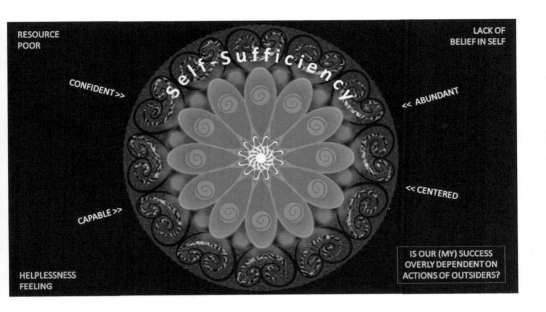

RESOURCE POOR

LACK OF BELIEF IN SELF

CONFIDENT >>

Self-Sufficiency

<< ABUNDANT

CAPABLE >>

<< CENTERED

HELPLESSNESS FEELING

IS OUR (MY) SUCCESS OVERLY DEPENDENT ON ACTIONS OF OUTSIDERS?

CLOSED-MINDED

CLEVER AND GLIB

PATIENT >>

Truthfulness

<< GRATEFUL

RECEPTIVE >>

<< SILENT

OVERLY LITERAL AND LOGICAL

IS OUR (MY) VIEWPOINT TOO FIXED AND LIMITING?

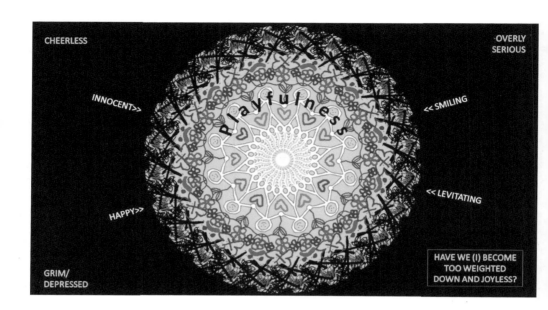

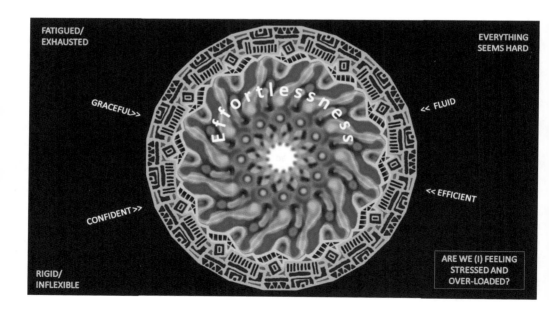

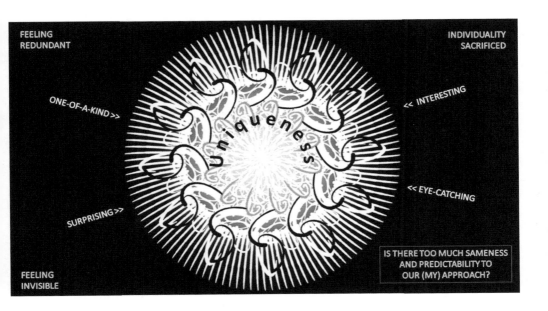

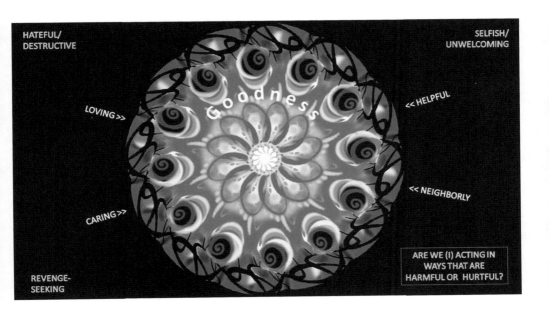

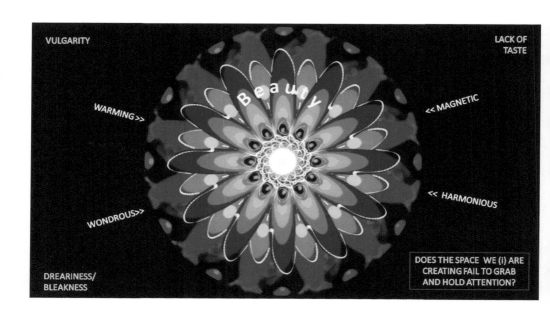

VULGARITY

LACK OF TASTE

WARMING >>

Beauty

<< MAGNETIC

<< HARMONIOUS

WONDROUS>>

DREARINESS/ BLEAKNESS

DOES THE SPACE WE (i) ARE CREATING FAIL TO GRAB AND HOLD ATTENTION?

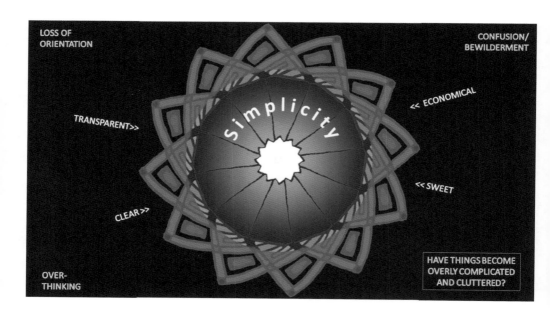

LOSS OF ORIENTATION

CONFUSION/ BEWILDERMENT

TRANSPARENT>>

Simplicity

<< ECONOMICAL

<< SWEET

CLEAR >>

OVER- THINKING

HAVE THINGS BECOME OVERLY COMPLICATED AND CLUTTERED?

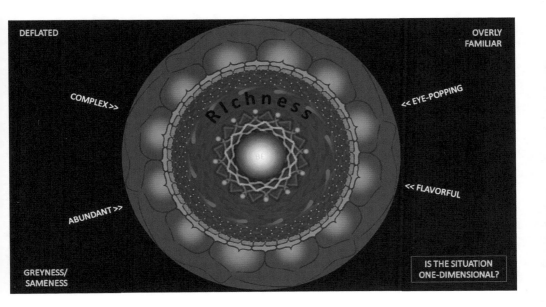

DEFLATED

OVERLY FAMILIAR

COMPLEX >>

<< EYE-POPPING

Richness

<< FLAVORFUL

BE

ABUNDANT >>

GREYNESS/ SAMENESS

IS THE SITUATION ONE-DIMENSIONAL?

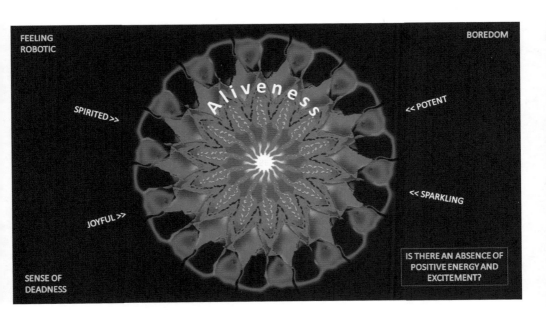

FEELING ROBOTIC

BOREDOM

SPIRITED >>

<< POTENT

Aliveness

<< SPARKLING

JOYFUL >>

SENSE OF DEADNESS

IS THERE AN ABSENCE OF POSITIVE ENERGY AND EXCITEMENT?

90

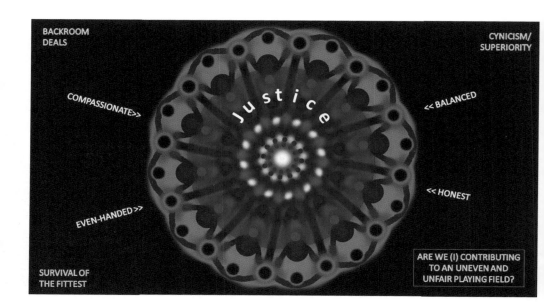

BACKROOM
DEALS

CYNICISM/
SUPERIORITY

COMPASSIONATE>>

Justice

<< BALANCED

<< HONEST

EVEN-HANDED >>

SURVIVAL OF
THE FITTEST

ARE WE (I) CONTRIBUTING
TO AN UNEVEN AND
UNFAIR PLAYING FIELD?

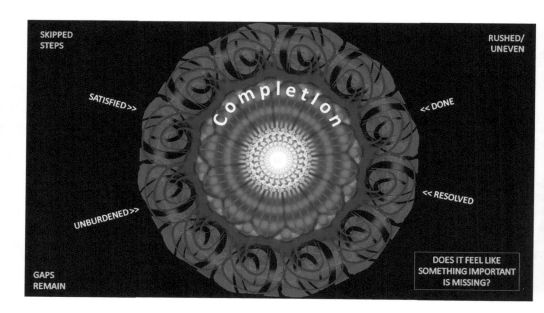

SKIPPED
STEPS

RUSHED/
UNEVEN

SATISFIED >>

Completion

<< DONE

<< RESOLVED

UNBURDENED >>

GAPS
REMAIN

DOES IT FEEL LIKE
SOMETHING IMPORTANT
IS MISSING?

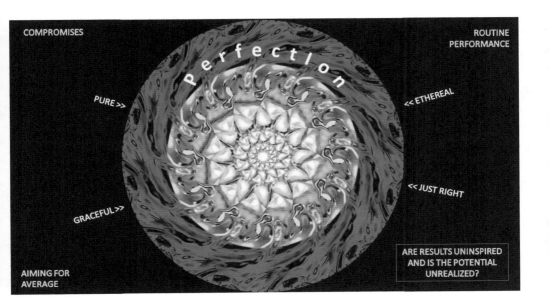

COMPROMISES

ROUTINE
PERFORMANCE

PURE >>

<< ETHEREAL

Perfection

<< JUST RIGHT

GRACEFUL >>

AIMING FOR
AVERAGE

ARE RESULTS UNINSPIRED
AND IS THE POTENTIAL
UNREALIZED?

IT'S THEM
VERSUS US

ISOLATION/
SEPARATION

HARMONIOUS >>

<< COUPLED

Wholeness

<< UNIFIED

AT-ONENESS >>

EITHER-OR
THINKING

IS OUR (MY)
MINDSET DIVISIVE
AND FRAGMENTED?

Selected References

Hoffman, Edward. *Future Visions: The Unpublished Papers of Abraham Maslow*. SAGE Publications, 1996.

Maslow, Abraham. *Toward a Psychology of Being*. D. Van Nostrand Company, 1968.

Maslow, Abraham. *Religions, Values, and Peak-Experiences*. Penguin Books, 1976.

Maslow, Abraham. *The Farther Reaches of Human Nature*. An Esalen Book, 1975.

Inspiration and, in some cases, short statements were drawn from the selected writings of:

David Aaron
A. H. Almaas
Yogi Bhajan
Brent Bill
Walter Brueggemann
Martin Buber
Deepak Choprah
Abraham Heschel
Frank Jones
J. Krishnamurti
Mary-Margaret Moore
Paramahansa Yogananda
Ram Daas
Ramana Maharishi
Bagwan Shree Rajneesh
Julius Stulman
Ken Wilber
Franklin Merrell-Wolff

Made in the USA
Charleston, SC
27 April 2014